DANCING WITH
THE BEAR

NEGOTIATING
THE SUPERINTENDENT
EMPLOYMENT CONTRACT

DR. RALPH BAKER

DANCING WITH
THE BEAR

NEGOTIATING
THE SUPERINTENDENT
EMPLOYMENT CONTRACT

Dancing with the Bear: Negotiating the Superintendent Employment Contract

©2018 Dr. Ralph Baker

ISBN 9780990410324

Library of Congress Control Number 2018947765

Contract Doctor logo: Gretchen Kamp, Graphic Designer
www.gretchenkamp.com 805.405.2474

Book design by Nancy Barnes, www.StoriesToTellBooks.com

DISCLAIMER

This book is not intended as a substitute for legal advice of an attorney.

The views, thoughts and opinions expressed are solely those of the author in his private capacity and do not in any way represent the views of the San Bernardino County Superintendent of Schools or the Team of District Governance Advisors.

The Publisher and the Author have made every attempt to provide the reader with accurate, timely, and useful information. However, given the rapid changes taking place in today's superintendent job market some of our information will inevitably change. The author makes no claims that using this information will guarantee the reader a superintendent employment contract.

The author shall not be liable for any losses or damages incurred in the process of following the advice in this book. No warranty may be created or extended by sales or promotional materials. The advice and strategies contained herein may not be suitable for every superintendent employment contract due to the diversity of individual state employment laws and regulations. This work is sold with the understanding that the author is not engaged in rendering legal, accounting, or professional services. If professional assistance is required the services of an educational attorney should be sought preferably from a state educational administration association. Neither the Publisher nor the Author shall be liable for damages arising from the information within this book. The fact that an organization or website is referred to in this work as a citation and/or potential source of future information does not mean that the Author or Publisher endorses the information the organization or website may provide or recommendations it may make. Further, readers should be aware that internet websites listed in this work may have changed or disappeared since this work was written and when it was read.

Printed in the United States of America

PUBLICITY RIGHTS

For information on publicity, author interviews, presentation, or subsidiary rights, contact Dr. Ralph Baker: indioralph@aol.com 760-514-8631

Delmar Publishing
Huntington Beach, CA
Drmlr@yahoo.com

DANCING WITH THE BEAR

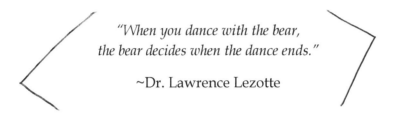

*"When you dance with the bear,
the bear decides when the dance ends."*

~Dr. Lawrence Lezotte

Once you sign that first superintendent employment contract you are *DANCING WITH THE BEAR!*

School boards are metaphorically the bear in the woods.

Before you rush into the educational forest,

Negotiate a comprehensive employment contract.

It will serve as your refuge

If the board becomes dysfunctional.

A bear out of control

Is not a pretty sight and not prone to listening.

Tread lightly and have your eyes wide open.

You're in their world now.

It is wise to treat them with the respect they rightfully deserve

And provide a wide path for them to walk.

Contents

ACKNOWLEDGEMENTS

Thank you to the following people who critically reviewed the text and provided invaluable feedback.

Richard Bray, District Governance Advisor
San Bernardino County Superintendent of Schools

Jan Gonzales, Superintendent
Victor Elementary School District

Dr. Mitch Hovey, District Governance Advisor
San Bernardino County Superintendent of Schools

Dr. Sherry Kendrick, District Governance Advisor
San Bernardino County Superintendent of Schools

Dr. Dale Marsden, Superintendent
San Bernardino City Unified School District

Dr. Reed Montgomery, Retired Superintendent
Plan Member Financial Services

Dr. Kegham Tashjian
Advisor to San Bernardino County Superintendent of Schools
and District Governance Advisors Team Lead
San Bernardino County Superintendent of Schools Office

Lloyd Wamhof
Association of California School Administrators
Member Assistance and Legal Support Team

Dr. Ron Williams, Superintendent
Victor Valley Union High School District

A Special Acknowledgement

Karen Baker, retired architectural draftsperson.

Devoted wife, who lived the experience and has a keen eye for detail.

Her tireless reading and re-reading was instrumental to this book's completion.

FOREWORD

When I read this book, I felt like I was replaying hundreds of conversations I've had personally with Ralph over the last decade of my career as superintendent. Dr. Baker welcomes you to one of the most volatile careers in American history, and offers the solution to your success in an industry where the average tenure of the CEO is less than 36 months. He's right to say superintendents see their initial contract with the board as an "inconsequential formality," aka, a Fatal Negotiating Mistake. He has written a book that is chock-full of strategies and negotiating tips that contain the most effective elements for the superintendent's contract. His 24 years as a superintendent (in the same district), and his track record of results, leading one of the state's highest performing high-poverty districts, makes his exhortation, "Trust Me," actually mean something.

And you can trust him when he says that the same level of thought and preparation you put into your interview needs to go into your employment contract. You can trust him when he says, "Failure to negotiate a comprehensive contract could result in your failure as a superintendent." You'll be clear on the fact that this initial seemingly self-interested focus of contract negotiations actually bridges the larger void of the district and community you have decided to serve.

"The employment contract is the cornerstone of success or failure of the superintendent."

Dr. Baker reminds us that we should never forget that the position of the superintendent has an unrivaled influence on public education, and it is our duty to protect the position, to ensure the organizations we serve deliver on their educational mission for students to reach the American dream. To achieve this outcome you will need a contract that clarifies roles and responsibilities, as well as expectations and accountability. Your contract will help you develop a positive working relationship with your board so that you can do your job and get results.

"This book is a must-read for every new and sitting superintendent."

Dr. Dale Marsden, Ed. D., Superintendent

San Bernardino City Unified School District, ADA 50,000

Testimonials

"As a new or experienced superintendent this book is invaluable in negotiating your contract! Dr. Baker has captured the important points and offered great tips with numerous anecdotes that enhance his message. More than negotiating a contract, this is a book on being an effective leader."

~Lloyd Wamhof, Association of California School Administrators

"Dr. Ralph Baker's practical knowledge and expertise levels the playing field for superintendents undertaking the most critical element of their professional career."

~Dr. Ron Williams, Superintendent

"I am extremely grateful to have had Dr. Baker's coaching. As a result I was able to negotiate with my board of trustees in a manner that was respectful, collegial, yet firm in holding fast to the content in the contract that would create clear expectations for my role as superintendent."

~Dr. Edwin Gomez, Superintendent

"When I was appointed superintendent, I was so thrilled I would have taken the job without a contract. Fortunately, I had a strong mentor in Dr. Baker. He shared his extensive skill and knowledge in superintendents' contracts and discussed the perfect fit for me. Looking back, I now understand the important points he made regarding my contract."

~Jan Gonzales, Superintendent

"I never imagined just how much I would come to rely on the strength of a solid contract. When I first got the job, I was happy to get the job. But as the game changed and I experienced a significant shift in board leadership, my contract served as my anchor during the storm. From evaluation to protocols to expectations, roles and responsibilities — every area distinctly and thoughtfully outlined gave me strength in times of crisis to do the right things in the right ways and to ensure my own sustainability — and the sustainability of the organization. I am forever indebted."

~Dr. Dale Marsden, Superintendent

"When I was offered a superintendent's position and entered into contract negotiations with the Board, I had no idea where to begin. Dr. Baker wrote items into my contract that never would have crossed my mind, and carefully explained the importance of each of those items. Now, thanks to Dr. Baker, I have been able to rely on that contract for my long-term financial benefit and my sustainability as a superintendent."

~Mike Hayhurst, Superintendent

ABOUT THE AUTHOR

Dr. Ralph Baker is a retired California superintendent of public schools who served 24 very successful years as a superintendent in one school district. His leadership brought about outstanding state test scores; excellent employee pay; high site discretionary dollars; and a strong ending balance.

Under his direction the schools received numerous state and national recognition awards. The very conservative community passed its first and other General Obligation Bonds to build schools.

He personally negotiated his own employment contract on ten occasions. Superintendents have sought his advice and counsel in drafting their employment contracts, and he has personally negotiated on behalf of superintendents.

Currently he serves as a District Governance Advisor for the San Bernardino County Superintendent of Schools Office. He works with a team of retired superintendents tasked with assisting school boards to fill vacant superintendent positions as well as working to facilitate high performing board-superintendent teams.

His interest in negotiating superintendent contracts grew as a result of a contract controversy at the end of his career. He made several avoidable blunders, and his intention was to learn from his mistakes and assist aspiring superintendents and school board members from making the same or similar errors.

He earned a Ph.D. in education from Claremont Graduate University, a M.A. in educational administration from California State University at San Bernardino, and a B.A. from the University of California at Riverside. He further holds elementary and secondary teaching credentials from the University of California at Riverside as well as an administrative services credential from California State University at San Bernardino.

Contact Information:

indioralph@aol.com

760.514.8631 (cell)

"He danced with the bear and retired on his terms."

About this Book

It is rare for a new superintendent to possess the skill and knowledge to effectively lead staff to achieve board direction. It is rare because a rookie superintendent doesn't have the experiential background to draw upon when considering the intricate leadership requirements needed within a comprehensive employment contract. They tend to view the contract offered by the board as an inconsequential formality and do not see the connection and impact it will have on their ability to lead the district. It is building a leadership foundation on sand.

With the information that follows the superintendent will enter negotiations with a direction and purpose. This book will serve to shape a contract that provides a solid foundation from which to lead a successful school district.

The enclosed material provides a foundation for aspiring superintendents to navigate the political landscape to negotiate a superintendent employment contract. It may also serve current superintendents looking to move to a new district or simply looking for some pointers to negotiate a successor contract with their current district.

Most importantly it provides an understanding of:

♦ What is contained within a comprehensive contract

♦ What are the "must haves"

♦ When you should walk away from an offer

♦ How to negotiate the contract

AN EXCELLENT COMPANION BOOK
Suggested Reading: *RULES OF THE GAME: How to Win a Job in Educational Leadership* by Dr. Marilou Ryder, 2016.

Introduction

SETTING THE STAGE

Think of yourself as an independent contractor. You will negotiate with the board an agreement to manage their district and to assist them with identifying and achieving their vision for student education. You have either had an excellent interview, and the board desires your skill and knowledge to lead their district, or you have had a superb career, and the board salutes your work by asking you to become superintendent.

With this in mind we will look at the employment contract. We want to take care in thinking through your contract, as for the most part you are on your own. This may very well be the first time in your career you have had to focus totally on yourself. We are used to serving others and being part of a team. You may have no problem with self-sacrifice, but now you must represent yourself and *not* sacrifice yourself in the political arena you are about to enter.

My goal is to walk you through the negotiating process in a conversational tone. I will take much liberty in this conversational tone, as I want to be as real as possible so that you go in to the negotiating process with your eyes wide open. You are about to enter a special group of individuals—superintendents. The position of superintendent, more than any other position in education, has the fastest turnover rate and is exposed to the highest risk of termination. You are about to take the ultimate risk in education and for that you are to be complimented. My desire is to minimize your risk of making a career-ending mistake.

WHAT THIS BOOK IS NOT

This book is not about how to secure a massive salary and benefit package or how to exert power over a school board. It is about fairness and teamwork. Keep in mind that you have spent a career within a work environment with professional standards, yet you are about to enter a work environment where the standard for *the board* is to win the next election. The employment contract is to secure your professional success within a political work environment.

LEADER SUCCESS

My definition of leadership is very basic. You have a direction and a plan to achieve it, buoyed by a set of core values to focus your decisions. Let me provide a personal example. For me, once the classroom door closes, the primary motivator for student learning is the skill and knowledge of the classroom teacher. As a leader I made a conscious decision to spend money on staff development as opposed to class size reduction. I was not opposed to class size reduction, I simply valued skill and knowledge as that can't be taken away, whereas class size reduction can be taken away with the next round of state budget cuts.

BOARDS OF EDUCATION

The title Board of Education is used interchangeably with Board of Trustees. The general qualifications to be elected to a school board are a candidate must be a U.S. citizen, at least 18 or 21 years old and live within the school district boundaries. They cannot be an employee of the district. School board members are the largest body of elected officials in the United States. Members are elected to serve 4 year terms and then must be reelected. They do not have term limits. They set the policy of the school district and hire and fire the superintendent. Policies are position statements of how they want the district managed and are a system of principles to guide board decisions.

Effective boards have a clear understanding of their role to set long term strategic direction for the district and allow the superintendent to develop a plan to achieve their direction. The board's role is to then monitor the progress of the superintendent's plan of action throughout the year.

Ineffective boards will confuse governance with management, and try to tell the superintendent what to do and how to do it. This is a board over-reaching their authority, and it is the reason for a comprehensive contract, to safeguard the superintendent's ability to manage the day to day decisions of the district.

Boards usually have 3, 5, or 7 board members, depending on the size of the district. The contract serves to clarify the roles of the board and superintendent, as role confusion will affect the board-superintendent team effectiveness. It takes a highly trained and skilled superintendent to facilitate board member interactions and to keep everyone focused on the future direction of the district.

New board members need special training to get them up to speed with the basics of being a board member, and superintendents need to work with the experienced board members to develop a program to train new board members in their role as a community leader. Some new board members naturally rise to the task, yet others crash and burn, as this may be the first time they have been in a position of power and they simply don't handle it well. My best advice is to treat them as you would your best friend. Praise them in public and politely inform them that you expect better of them in private. Sometimes this works, but at other times they go over the cliff. In those cases we let the next election run its course, as voters usually pick up on such board member antics.

WELCOME TO THE ROLLER COASTER RIDE

A roller coaster ride can be terrifying for a child and fun for an adult. You are about to hop on the grandest roller coaster ride of your professional life, so let's approach it as an adult and smooth out the highs and lows along the way.

CHAPTER 1

FATAL NEGOTIATING MISTAKE

"Once you squander an opportunity you can never get it back."

~Navy Captain Michael Abrashoff, 2002

THE ORIGINAL SIN

The importance of the contract is to provide a framework to allow you longevity on the job, so that you can lead the district and provide positive change to the educational program for students. Of all the negotiating mistakes that are made, none is more harmful to the longevity of the superintendent than quickly signing the original contract a board presents, without having a counter contract offer prepared in advance. This original contract may set the stage for communication problems between the superintendent and board as a result of fuzzy contract language, leading to role confusion.

HERE'S HOW IT HAPPENS

You have been fortunate enough to have been invited to interview with the board on a Saturday morning. Saturdays are best, as there will be no prying eyes to see the candidates. Employees will not be milling about, and you will have the board's total attention, as things are more relaxed on the weekend. At the end of the interview the search consultant informs you that you should wait around the area, as you are a front runner and may be called back to speak with the board.

THE BOARD SELECTS YOU!

Later that afternoon you receive a call that the board would like to meet with you again to offer you a contract. You meet with the board for a "grip and grin" session, and they inform you that they want you as the new superintendent. They further state that on *this* Wednesday they have scheduled a Special Board Meeting to introduce you to the community and staff.

Note the timeline: 4 days later. This is way too quick to review, understand the implications of contract language, and finally to negotiate a contract.

The search consultant walks you to your car and hands you a copy of the contract the board would like for you to review and sign before Wednesday night. You are assured this is a good contract. Most new candidates feel pressure to sign this contract to make a good impression on the board, staff, and community. The new superintendent excitedly signs the contract, thinking *"What could possibly go wrong?"*

JUST A SECOND: LET'S REWIND THIS SCENARIO

In this scenario, prior to the interview you drafted your contract proposal, reflecting your leadership style and your lifestyle. You have identified your "must haves" as well as identifying your "walk-aways" that would make you decline a contract.

You are the consummate professional and you don't emotionally react to the tight timeline or the consultant's push for you to sign the contract. You thank the consultant for the contract offer and inform the consultant, *"I will carefully review the offer."* Then you hand the consultant your contract proposal for the board's review and inform the consultant, *"I think it best if I am not introduced to the community until the contract has been negotiated and signed. I trust the board will agree."*

POISE UNDER STRESS

At this point you need to consider that the board may counter by informing you this is a "take it or leave it" contract offer. They don't want to negotiate.

Your opportunity is only possible if you have thought through your leadership needs and developed your contract in advance.

Note: "Take it or leave it" is not always take it or leave it. First, never need a job so badly you would sell your professional career to get it. Relax, take a breath and respond as follows:

♦ One way to say "thanks, but no thanks" is, "I'm looking for a board-superintendent team. If they change their minds and want to work as a team, I'd be interested in negotiating the contract."

♦ If you take their offer without further negotiation, my suggestion would be to ONLY take it for the experience you will gain as this Board will never be a long term employment proposition. They want to own you! From day one be looking for the next opportunity.

♦ If they do negotiate, some board members will be upset and frustrated with your requests. Your goal is to be calm and work through the issues to reach a mutually agreeable contract. You will achieve a measure of respect, as they were not able to own you.

REMEMBER WHEN YOU WERE A TEACHER

As you read this book, think of how you taught your students. Now think of how you would have been impacted if you had to deal directly with five board members, all of whom are receiving calls from upset students and parents. Board questions would have gone as follows:

"Why did you give that assignment? Wouldn't something else have been more appropriate?"

"What were you thinking, giving my next door neighbor's child a detention?"

"Are you still using that outdated textbook?"

"I don't feel it is appropriate for you to say such and such to students."

Just think of being bombarded with questions that you have to spend time researching, thinking through and responding to. Such is the life of a superintendent. The more defined the contract, the better board-superintendent team understanding of your respective roles, and fewer frivolous questions to answer. This alone will provide more time to develop strategies to move the education program forward.

CHAPTER 2

ASK FOR WHAT YOU WANT

"Successful people take 100% responsibility for everything they experience in life."

~Jack Canfield, 2005

ASK FOR ADVICE

Contact some of the these resources to help you in this process:

♦ Your state administrators association

♦ Your current superintendent

♦ The county superintendent

♦ Other area superintendents

♦ The search firm

YOUR CONTRACT IS LIKE A TICKING TIME BOMB

Most rookie superintendents have never negotiated a contract for themselves. They simply are at the mercy of the board's attorney or search consultant. Imagine you are attempting to defuse a bomb. If you haven't done this before, it would be in your best interest to seek advice from a BOMB expert. Your contract is like that bomb. Don't get blown away because of ignorance. *Seek advice!*

GOT GAME?

In the beginning we don't feel worthy to ask for anything, as we haven't yet accomplished anything as a superintendent. As time goes by, we don't recognize the different skill set that we have acquired that is needed to lead, nor do we want to self-promote our work to the board. We are busy promoting the work of our management team and staff members to our detriment. Therefore, most of us don't "have game."

During my second year of being a superintendent a board member stated, *"I don't know what you do."* I didn't know how to respond with a quick quip, so I stood there feeling foolish.

> *The Board president asked the member, "Did you like the district before he was here?"*
>
> *She responded, "No."*
>
> *The president said, "Do you like it now?"*
>
> *Her response was, "Yes."*
>
> *The board president finished the discussion by saying, "Well, that is what he does."*

This would have been acceptable if the puzzled board member would have given it some thought, and more importantly, if I would have followed up with board training on the importance of leadership and exactly what a leader does. I didn't have game, so with the next problem in the district, this same board member came to me and stated, "Just go out there and do what you do best—smile at people." *REALLY?* She didn't have a clue as to what I did on the job, and it was my fault. *"I don't know what you do."*

How would I answer that question today? Here's what I'd say.

"I develop a plan to coordinate the actions of all schools and district departments to achieve the board's direction and vision. I do this by implementing collaborative systems to monitor, inform, evaluate and recognize performance."

This is my description; other successful superintendents will have developed their own conclusions.

Most importantly, I would have:

♦ Negotiated my specific duties as a superintendent in the employment contract, so that the board understood what I did as a superintendent, and what they are to do as a board.

♦ Conducted an annual workshop with the board to review, not negotiate, my contract, so that we would not experience role confusion.

♦ At the annual workshop, I would have a third party facilitator to provide balance to the discussion. If it is just you and the board, it can become you against a board member.

SUPERINTENDENT PROBLEM

I have found that many superintendents prefer to avoid discussing their contract, as this may cause board members to question it. They would rather attempt to slide it through the board every three or four years with no changes or fanfare. *The employment contract is the cornerstone of success or failure of the superintendent.*

View negotiating the employment contract as the first issue you and the board will work through together, to form a more effective team. There will be disagreements and misunderstandings, and this is normal in negotiations. The deciding factor in the negotiation process will be your ability to compromise and reach an acceptable agreement, and the board will learn to respect your negotiating skill. *If you sign the first contract the Board puts in front of you, you are putting your professional career at risk.*

At the beginning of your contract: item #1 is Superintendent, Chief Executive Officer, and secretary to the Board. This clearly defines your role. There are times when individual board members refuse to accept that you are the CEO. Having this language in your contract clarifies the issue.

The superintendent employment contract forms the basis of the professional working relationship between the Board of Education and the superintendent. It is the cornerstone for your success or failure as a superintendent. *The Board will hold you responsible for problems. Therefore you need to define the authority you have to execute your leadership decisions to prevent problems.*

Success develops as a result of clearly defined roles of the board as well as the superintendent, and an economic package that provides for the financial security of the superintendent and family. This allows the superintendent to be totally focused on leading the district without distraction.

CEO: CLEARLY DEFINE YOUR ROLE

We were never trained to feel special or to believe that we were special- perhaps we're not- but the position of superintendent is special.

"I'm nobody! Who are you?

Are you nobody, Too?

Then there is a pair of us- don't tell

They'd banish us you know…."

~Emily Dickinson, 1891

WELCOME TO THE FISHBOWL

Whether or not you believe you are special is not the point. You will now be in a community fishbowl. People will know who *you* are without you knowing who *they* are. It comes with the territory of being the superintendent. The citizens will expect that you will be the consummate professional, fully prepared to advance the education of the youth of the community.

GIVE THE POSITION THE RESPECT IT DESERVES

The position of superintendent has the greatest impact on education within a district.

> *"The position of superintendent has twice the impact on student achievement than a whole school reform effort, and superintendent longevity on the job has a positive impact on student achievement starting as early as year two"* (Waters & Marzano, 2006).

OWN THIS FACT

We are not teachers. We are not protected by being a member of a union. We are a stand-alone commodity of the board. We are their only employee, in the most vulnerable position in education.

> *"The superintendency is the least stable and secure position in education"* (Metzger, 1997).

The stability of the superintendent is important to student learning and organizational success.

> *"There is a positive relationship between superintendent tenure and student achievement"* (Caplan, 2010).

Superintendent failure is caused by ambiguous contract language that doesn't clearly state their authority.

WHAT DECISIONS CAN YOU MAKE WITHOUT BOARD APPROVAL?

Ambiguity on this issue invites individual board members, staff, and community embers to drive a wedge between the board and superintendent by confusing board-superintendent authority. This results in board over-reach followed by the board going out of control.

Let me provide an example: I had a new board member who was pushed by a community member with a problem he felt I didn't resolve in his favor. He pushed on this new board member, as he was his neighbor. He demanded to know, "Aren't you the board member? Aren't you the boss of the superintendent?" The new board member came to me and repeated what his neighbor had asked him, as well as half-asking me for my opinion. I stated, "Yes, you are the board member, and a member of a board that takes three votes to direct me to do something that does not violate my contract."

Thank goodness I had this language in my contract!

I further added, "My contract states that I direct the day to day management of the district, not the board." I informed the new board member that in the future, when you are asked this same or similar question, I would suggest this response: *"As a board, we have negotiated a contract with the superintendent that gives him the authority to make this decision."* I further explained that the follow-up question will likely be, "Then why do we need a board?" I suggested he respond, "We monitor and evaluate the performance of the superintendent." I added that when you explain it in these terms they will not like you at that moment. You hope they will learn to respect you over time. *When board and superintendent understand their authority, it makes the district more effective for staff and students.*

"WHY DON'T YOU ASK TEACHERS TO GIVE UP TENURE RIGHTS?"

♦ There are superintendents who don't want to ask for anything the teachers don't receive.

♦ There are board members who never want to give the superintendent anything different than what the teachers receive.

I had a board member ask me how he could defend the board paying for a tax sheltered annuity (TSA) for me, the superintendent, as it was something the teachers didn't receive. I said, "Why don't you ask the teachers union to give up their tenure rights, and I will negotiate for *some* teachers a TSA. As a superintendent, I don't have employment protection, and that is a huge benefit-for teachers. That is why they don't receive what superintendents receive, as the superintendent is the most exposed to termination and teachers are protected."

> "*Incoherence causes board-superintendent dysfunction*"
> (Dawson, Quinn, 2000).

The purpose of this book is to explain the subtleties of negotiating a contract. As a result you will view the conflict of negotiations as the normal give and take of a natural healthy exchange of ideas. If it ends with anger or hurt, you did it wrong. Anger resulting in animosity of the board toward the superintendent is dangerous to the professional life of the superintendent. There will always be individual board members with issues, and don't let them hook you into their game of conflict. Some board members thrive on crisis conflict and everything is a crisis to them. Don't fixate on them. Refocus attention to the full board. Ask, "Do any of you have this concern?"

CONFLICT IS NORMAL

Anger, fear, hurt, sarcasm, and suspicion have no place in the life of the superintendent. It is always wise to bear in mind that conflict is normal and natural as long as you, the superintendent, have one goal and that is for both sides to be able to accept and live with the contract. It is paramount as superintendent that in any conflict you have an absolute belief that all sides will be able to work through the conflict to a mutually agreeable resolution. Anger, fear, hurt, sarcasm, or suspicion have no place in the life of the superintendent.

A HEALTHY DOSE OF PARANOIA IS A GOOD THING

Never engage or explain your reasoning to an argumentative board member. Let the other board members handle that situation or turn to the other Board members and respond to them. A good strategy when an argumentative board member confronts you at a board meeting with a problem is to turn to the other board members and ask, "Do any of you share this same concern?"

Always remember to trust and be a little paranoid, as *some* people *are* out to get you. Forget that at your peril. I had one board member who was famous for stating, "No one forced you to become superintendent." She would say this whenever she thought I was asking for more than what I should receive. Never confront an argumentative board member, as it is futile. Just listen for understanding.

She was a good person and an excellent employee for her boss. Let's think through her argument. She wanted me to sit down, shut up and take what the board told me, or quit. Did she think that is how our teachers and classified employees behave at the negotiating table?

TERRIBLE ADVICE

Mark Twain stated, "It is better to keep your mouth closed and let people think you are a fool than to open it and remove all doubt." Yet when it comes to your contract this is terrible advice.

You want to ask the foolish questions before *you sign your contract.* Which is worse: not asking questions and remaining ignorant, or asking questions and getting your contract right for your leadership style? If you have small children at home, be able to look them in the eye and say, *"I have your back and your future too."* Always keep in your mind that you are negotiating for their protection. They trust you. You need to think of them before you negotiate away their future.

Superintendents who are most successful interact with their professional organization and other superintendents. They ask questions, admit what they don't know, challenge the process, and in short, actively engage in designing their own contract based on their needs. They let the board know how much they appreciate the original contract offer, but they will need to review the contract before signing.

> *"If you can't run with the big dogs stay on the porch!"*
>
> ~John Madden, former professional football coach

It seems those superintendents who have problems prefer to sign the first contract offered by the board without question or understanding. They keep their contract under wraps and stay to themselves. It's a contract they don't own, and they definitely do not understand the sophistication of the detail of a comprehensive contract. They say, *"I don't want to start the job in conflict with the board."*

Most superintendents wait for the board to offer their contract and then sign it without question, as they don't want conflict with their new employer. Let's think for a second. Do you believe the board sends the teacher's association a contract, fully expecting that they will not read it, sign off on it, and then exclaim to the board, *"Oh, thank you!"* The board understands negotiating a contract comes with the territory, with teachers and with classified employees. Yet they tend to have less patience with superintendent negotiations. Why? Because you represent one vote. Teachers and classified employees represent many more votes—it's politics.

I am steadfastly convinced new superintendents could lead longer, and more effectively with less stress, if they negotiated a comprehensive contract with roles clearly defined. I worked with one superintendent who had a cut and paste contract gathered from a few superintendents. I had a hard time understanding it and wondered if the board's legal counsel had even reviewed it. Needless to say, after several issues with the board, the superintendent left the district after one year.

WHAT WILL YOU HAVE ACCOMPLISHED FIVE YEARS FROM NOW?

"You always told us where we would be in five years, and we got there!"

~Mike Davis, former board member

Five years from now you will have improved the academic achievement of your students as measured by state exams. You will have a financially secure district with well paid staff and a comprehensive contract that allowed all this to develop over time.

CHAPTER 3

NEGOTIATE THE CONTRACT

"Knowing how to negotiate constructively is an essential skill for any career."

~Johnson, D., & Johnson, F. (2000)

THE BASICS

Let's start by looking at a typical scenario for negotiating a superintendent employment contract. *The board presents their contract to the superintendent candidate and the candidate signs it.* Is there any wonder why we have superintendent turnover? In my opinion this is why we have a pretty regular turnover in superintendents. Well it is time to be a CEO. You need a direction, a plan to achieve it, and a contract that defines your values to lead one of the most educated work forces in the world.

FIRST QUESTION FOR THE SEARCH CONSULTANT

"Are my contract requests going to be new to the board?" If a board has never negotiated an item or items for previous superintendents, this will require careful negotiations, as it will be a radical concept to them.

The negotiating "formula" is 1) respectful listening and 2) paraphrasing their concerns.

For the board, this is going to be viewed as an out of the box request, or in the words of Tim Waters (2005), "It represents a Type II change". It simply is not in their thinking; it's a radical concept. Don't let this faze you. Please remember—you are not a teacher, you are the *leader* of teachers, and your contract will be materially different because of this fact.

10 BASIC NEGOTIATING RULES

The average superintendent will negotiate the first contract through the search consultant for the board. The search consultant is more than likely a retired superintendent, so they know the job you are seeking. The search consultant will be pulling for you, but remember, they are paid by the board. The board will have thought through the parameters of their offer with the search consultant. In short, they *own* their proposal, and will not want to change it, as it is difficult to get 3, 5, or 7 board members to reach agreement.

With this in mind, I suggest you enter negotiations with the realistic attitude that there will be disagreements, and you need to steel yourself to this reality. Otherwise the board will start referring to you as "Matt," as in "doormat."

1. Prepare your contract before your first interview and get it into the board's hands as soon as possible to have them negotiate from your proposal (Giang, 2018).

2. Identify and rank order your contract goals, and state them upfront (Nisen, 2014).

3. Draft a pre-negotiations memo and attach it to the contract, stating your contract goals (Baker, 2018).

4. Be open and friendly. Get into a conversational tone by asking about the search consultant's career (Giang, 2018).

5. Have coffee or shot of expresso, as this has been found to bolster your backbone, so that you will not cave at the first sign of resistance (Giang, 2018).

6. During negotiations show emotion: smile, frown, and flinch where appropriate (Giang, 2018).

7. Maintain eye contact. Don't look down or shy away. Calmly look the other party in the eye without blinking (Nisen, 2014).

8. Start with a salary higher than you want. It will serve as an anchor throughout negotiations, driving negotiations your way even if you settle for less than you asked (Giang, 2018).

9. Provide as much data and research as possible to support your contract requests, as it makes the other party open to persuasion (Giang, 2018).

10. If the board is stalling with making a decision., inform the board through the search consultant that you are seriously considering removing yourself from consideration for the position as you need to "focus attention on your current position" or that you are "seriously considering other offers." If you receive no immediate response or an acceptable explanation, follow through by withdrawing (Giang, 2018).

SEVEN BASIC NEGOTIATING STRATEGIES

STRATEGY #1 NO QUICK CONTRACT SIGNING

Try to have impulse control. *But the board will get upset!* Yes, *some* board members will get upset with this action. We are talking about what it takes for you to lead a district without distractions. There are those board members who believe, "You will do as we direct you to do!"

This is about you and what you need to be successful. The contract you are about to sign means everything to your future. *Study* it carefully, and respond appropriately as to your needs. Remaining polished and poised will earn the board's respect.

Do negotiations ever fail? *Yes*. And then the contract isn't signed, and the board looks for a new candidate, and you dodged a bullet, because it wasn't right for you. The board wants you? Once you sign the contract, the board *owns* you. You are "dancing with the bear." *Before* you sign the contract, the board wants you. This is a powerful position to be in, and most superintendents waste their leadership impact with an attitude of, "I'll accept whatever the board believes is fair."

When a superintendent signs a contract without carefully understanding what they need to lead a district, the board usually ends up owning the superintendent, as there are no safeguards in the contract. The superintendent could end up being a leader in name only, not a leader adding value to student education.

STRATEGY #2 NEGOTIATE YOUR CONTRACT AND YOUR INTEREST

Have your contract prepared before you interview.

- ♦ Some superintendent candidates believe this is bad luck. I go by the adage, "The harder I work, the luckier I get." So be prepared! You don't want to lead a district with an attitude of "luck, fate and chance."

- It is *your* leadership skill and knowledge that is most important.

- When you are contacted with an offer of the position, let them know you will forward *your contract requests* for their review.

- You want to negotiate from your contract, as opposed to negotiating from theirs, as you will draft your contract based on what will make you most successful as the CEO of the district.

STRATEGY #3 LISTEN TO THEIR OFFER AND CONCERNS

The more you can get them to explain their reasons for something, and the calmer you stay, trust and respect will start to develop between you and the board. A good listening strategy is to ask, *"Why does the board want this?"* I can't emphasize this enough. If you have spent quality time thinking through what you want in a contract, you will be invested in it. In short, you will own it, and you won't want to give up anything. Typically, in these moments people will revert to defending, persuading and arguing their positions, (Goulston, 2009). Don't fall into the trap of responding defensively, such as, "I'm only asking for this because…."

Flip the script by *asking questions* (Robertson, 2014). "What are the board's concerns with my request?" Let them fully explain, and then say, "Let me mark this point and initial it as your concern." You want to find out if this a one person issue, or a full board issue. You then ask them to go through the entire contract, stipulating their concerns per each item. It can be a slow process when negotiating a full contract, but it will save time in the long run of your career if everyone knows their role and if you develop an ongoing process to communicate your respective roles.

STRATEGY #4 GO SLOW TO GO FAST

Methodically go through the contract, noting where both sides have complete agreement, and where there is a concern of the board. By going slowly through the contract and gaining clarity in the beginning, this process allows you to make faster decisions with less aggravation later, as you begin leading the District.

- ♦ If you find you have a problem with their position, ask to set it aside and come back to it at the end. You want quick wins at the start, so look for agreement.

- ♦ When you are all done, that is the time to go back through the problem areas for the board.

- ♦ Question, and question again, their concerns. Sometimes you will hear, "The board will never agree to a... (example: a 4-year contract; TSA amount; moving expenses; super-majority vote for termination" or whatever issue they have.) Be calm and respond honestly, "That would be a problem for me, and I respectfully ask the board to reconsider their offer. I feel we are close to agreeing to the contract terms, and I don't want this to prevent us from reaching an agreement."

If there are several issues, it is okay to schedule another meeting after the representative has been able to meet with the full board.

As you can see, this could take some time. The *problem* is that search firms usually have a tight deadline to fill the position, and you will feel pressure to sign. *Relax.* Your message is to state, "It is best that we get this contract right before I begin work, as opposed to after I start." *Being patient could mean the difference between success and termination.*

STRATEGY #5 ASK FOR WHAT YOU WANT

Keep stating what you want until you receive a firm "No." Most people are afraid to do this. Until someone says *No*, you are not asking for enough (Goulston, 2009). Example: A superintendent friend developed cancer, and informed the board they would need to begin a search for a new superintendent. The board stalled, and after a year the superintendent informed them of his last day on the job. The board then promptly began the search, and the current superintendent was surprised when they offered a starting salary $50,000 above what he was making. After all he had done for them, and especially after staying on through his cancer treatments, this was the thanks he got! I questioned him, "Did you ask for more?" "He said, "No." *If you don't ask for it, you won't get it!*

STRATEGY #6 FULL BOARD, OR SINGLE MEMBER ISSUE?

There is always a board member who will have an issue with your requests.

- ♦ The negotiator for the board will present that the board has a problem with a contract request.

- ♦ Ask if it is a single board member issue, a majority board issue, or a full board issue.

- ♦ You will want to learn the reason, but don't give up on your request—not until you receive a firm "No" from the *board majority*.

- ♦ Even if the problem is a full board issue, don't give up too quickly.

- ♦ You will want to learn of their reasoning, so don't let their negotiator get you to back off when they state, "The board will never agree to that." The negotiator for the board will attempt to move to the next issue.

♦ You want to listen to their reasoning. If this is important to you, simply state, "This is important to me, for this reason." Add, "I think the board can do better than this offer, and I would like for you to present it to them in this manner."

Sometimes when a board knows you have a major objection, they will negotiate a better deal. Remember, they have thought through their position as a board, and now they have to consider the requests from the superintendent's perspective.

KNOW WHAT YOU WANT, ASK FOR WHAT YOU WANT

When I was negotiating a superintendent contract renewal with the board's attorney, he presented language changing Superintendent Termination. Specifically, he wanted to change a super-majority vote to a simple majority for termination with cause and without cause. My first question was to ask, "Is this a full board request?" He responded, "No, it was a request from one board member." Our response, "We have no interest in making this change, especially since the superintendent has had no issues causing the board to desire this change."

The attorney was fine with leaving it as is. My point is that when the attorney presented the request, he made it appear the full board wanted this change, and when we discovered it was a single board member issue, we objected and prevailed. Usually board problems stem from something the former superintendent received or didn't receive, or that the board has never offered, or the teachers don't receive.

STAY ON MESSAGE

"I want to stay focused on leading the district: To do this we need a clear description of our board-superintendent responsibilities."

"My interest is to financially protect my family: I'm interested in keeping my family financially safe."

STRATEGY #7 KNOW YOUR DEAL BREAKERS

> *"If you cannot walk away from a contract offer, then you must accept what the other is willing to give."*
> ~Johnson, D. & Johnson, F, (2000)

What would cause you to say, "Thanks, but no thanks?"

♦ Two years or less contract offer

♦ Fuzzy evaluation process

♦ Termination process requiring only a majority vote and vague cause of action

♦ Any buy-out provision that must be negotiated

♦ Language that states you must have board approval before you make a decision

A Critical Point: Don't walk away until you provide the board with an opportunity to address your concern.

WHEN IN DOUBT, TRY HONESTY

♦ Don't threaten to walk away

♦ Simply state, "This is a problem for me."

♦ Ask, "How can we rectify the issue?"

An assistant superintendent informed me she was offered the vacant superintendent position and sent me the board contract offer for review. I rewrote it, and when she presented it to the board, they explained their contract as a "take it or leave it offer," and she had until 5:00 pm to sign or they would find another candidate. I advised her if she took the job, do so understanding she would be looking for her next job from day one; she would only get experience from this job. She did not look for a new job, as she thought she could make it work, and they let her go after a year.

NEGOTIATING TIPS

♦ *Expect counter proposals* from the board, as this tends to create greater buy-in to the final contract.

♦ Learn the art of "the flinch" a visible reaction to something you don't like (Robertson, 2014).

♦ A good counter-question is, **"Is this the best the board can do?"** You will either get a rationalization of why or an immediate concession (Robertson, 2014).

♦ If there is no response, request that the full board review the contract to see what they can do differently, as you expect better for your spouse or family.

DON'T COUNTER TOO LOW

♦ Successful people ask for what they want and negotiate until they hear a hard, unanimous, No.

♦ To create buy-in, get them to tell you things about their offer and practice reflecting back what they say. Mirror their feelings, without your personal emotions—even if you vehemently disagree (Goulston, 2009).

The board has thought through their proposal based on their needs. Once they understand you have a problem with an area of the contract, there are times they will re-consider their position. It is about listening, patience, and fixed eye contact to show you mean business–in a nice way.

Example: The board's counter is that the board will never agree to this request. Respond "Why is that?" calmly, with one or both palms turned up to invite a response. After their response, and your reflection, you could ask, "What can we do to get past the objection?" Or, "What would you advise to help the board to get past their objection?" If they won't budge, ask to move on and come back to this later. Look for small wins where both sides agree, and give a little early on, if the board has a problem with an item.

DON'T TRIM YOUR SALARY REQUEST TO THE BONE

Most superintendents want to trim their salary request on their initial contract proposal. You can always lower your request, but you will never be able to increase it. Start high, as most boards will want to take some away from your request. Or, *surprise!* they agree to your request.

Work through NO. If the board is absolutely steadfastly against something in your contract that you would like to have, never fold and submit until you take them through the process. Question, "Is this a single board member issue?" "What is the board's issue?" Restate your position: "This is important to me. Is this the best the board can do?"

NEGOTIATIONS ARE IRRATIONAL

- ♦ Negotiate from facts, not feelings (Stim).

- ♦ Mentally remove yourself from the situation. Sit in the balcony and be an observer.

- ♦ Don't get emotionally hijacked. Imagine you are protected by a Teflon shield.

WRAP IT UP AND PUT A BOW ON IT

- ♦ "I know our negotiations were difficult, and I want to thank you for sticking through this process. We were able to reach a successful conclusion that both my family and I appreciate. I've learned to respect your positions as Board Members as a result of our negotiations, and I thank you."

- ♦ "I want to sincerely apologize for any problems I may have caused anyone during negotiations, as that was not my intent. I genuinely hope that no one took anything personally, as I always separate the issue from the person in reaching an acceptable compromise."

FINAL TIP-PRACTICE NEGOTIATING

I suggest you role play "negotiating" just as you would prepare for a job interview. You want to make your list of your contract goals and practice working through "No" scenarios. For example, let's say your contract goals are: a four year contract; super-majority vote for termination; and 5% TSA/ Life Insurance Payment.

One strategy is to *bundle* like items. I would take the three priorities stated above, put them together, and start by having the board/search consultant answer questions such as: "What exactly is the board's issue with these items? "

Go from active listening to sharing your needs. After you have carefully listened to and rephrased their concerns, now is the time to state your needs and wants. This is when and where you bring in your information to close the deal.

State your position: *"These items are important to me. As we know, the superintendent is most exposed to termination, and I would like financial and employment protection in the event a new board is elected. I am not a teacher with tenure rights, and I want the confidence to know the board wants me to be protected so that I can lead with few distractions."*

If the board refuses to budge, ask, *"Is this the best the board can do? Would they consider giving me a super-majority vote for termination during the first two years of the contract for some needed protection as well as 3% for a TSA/Life insurance?"* The next fall-back position would be, *"Would they agree to 1% TSA/ Life Insurance?"* The point is to negotiate and not cave at the first "No." Be persistent.

"Successful people ask for what they want and state what they don't want."

~Jack Canfield, (2005)

CHAPTER 4

COMPREHENSIVE CONTRACT DEFINED

Rule of thumb: The larger the district, the larger the salary and benefit package.

Why is this the rule? The larger the district, the more responsibility and the more people the superintendent must oversee and manage. There are more problems, as well as issues, both within the district as well as within the community. The larger the district, the more organizations within the community will be going after the superintendent from day one, as they wanted a person who represented their group, and you aren't that person. It is nothing personal, just politics.

In small districts, the superintendent wears many hats and has numerous challenges. Unfortunately, these districts do not have the finances to provide an economic package that protects the superintendent, yet they will provide one or two benefits. First they provide invaluable experience in learning the many functions of the position. Second, some superintendents thrive on the smallness of a community where they can interact and get to know students, their families, and the community. It becomes a fit and they may stay long term.

In California there is an exception to this rule, known as a Basic Aid District. When a small district's property tax exceeds the state Local Control Funding Formula, they will have more dollars per student to budget.

THE BASICS OF A COMPREHENSIVE CONTRACT

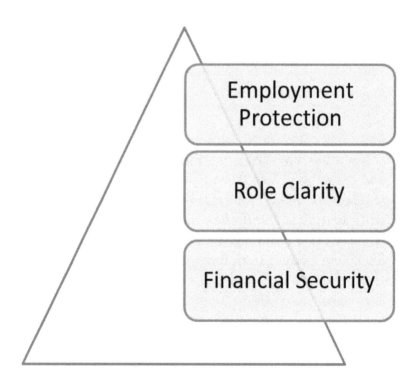

EMPLOYMENT PROTECTION

TERM

You want the maximum term allowed by law. Why?

- ♦ "To lead with confidence; I need security for my family."

- ♦ "I want everyone to know that the full board has confidence in my ability to successfully lead this district."

Most boards want to offer a contract below the maximum term allowed:

- ♦ *For me that is a **DEAL BREAKER**. The board should have done their homework well enough to know how you lead and the direction you want to take the district- That's on them.*

- ♦ *If you accept a contract for less than the maximum term, ask to put in the contract language a statement that if you receive a satisfactory evaluation, the board shall offer a maximum term contract at the next negotiations.*

- ♦ *A 2-year or less contract offer is definitely a **DEAL BREAKER**. It is an insult to leadership. It means the board thinks so little of the superintendent that they will consider terminating you at each and every board meeting.*

TERMINATION

"I want the confidence to know that a board will not be able to arbitrarily terminate me with my first mistake."

A CONTRACT MISTAKE COST A SUPERINTENDENT HIS CAREER

A sitting superintendent wanted to apply for a larger district. The board president informed him if he didn't get he job, he will be fired. He didn't get the new position, and he was fired. He didn't work in education again!

There are dysfunctional boards that expect you to be at their beck and call for life, or until they get tired of you and tell you to go away. If this is important to you, require language stating you have the right to seek a new position without threat of termination.

There are two primary forms of termination within a superintendent contract:

♦ Termination for cause

♦ Termination without cause (buyout)

TERMINATION FOR CAUSE

The following is paraphrased from a School Boards Association's sample superintendent contract. The usual board language would include:

The board may act to terminate the superintendent for cause on a *majority vote* of the board for the following *primary* reasons:

    a. Neglect of duty
    b. Breach of contract
    c. Any other legally permissible reason

The superintendent is the district's most visible representative and is required to maintain higher standards of personal conduct than any other employee, and shall avoid situations that might reflect negatively on the District.

The board may also have contract language under "General Duties" stating:

The superintendent shall perform, *at the highest level of competence*, all services, duties and obligations required by the contract, job description, laws, regulations and policies *and as otherwise directed by the board.*

EVALUATION LINKED TO TERMINATION

Now let's add to the mix evaluation language:

The board shall meet annually to establish the superintendent's goals and objectives. At the discretion of the board they *may* include input by the superintendent.

The board shall provide the evaluation instrument.

> *Boards are looking for God — on a good day.*
> *(Lewis, 2003)*

First, remember the board wants to protect their district and community from a superintendent's negligence, and this is the reason behind this *top down* contract language. What do I mean by "top down" contract language? The following details how a board can own a superintendent. As a board, they decide on your goals and objectives and the evaluation instrument. Also you must perform at the highest level of competence, *in their opinion.* In short, you will do what they direct you to do, when they tell you to, and how they tell you to. First you have to perform at the highest levels of competence. *Who makes this determination?* It is in the opinion of the majority of the board, unfortunately.

> *"School board member* subjective *evaluations of the superintendent's performance predicted turnover, but district performance did not." Andersen & Grissom, (2012).*

This simply means the average board releases superintendents on their feelings, not on performance. It is a slippery slope. *If the only way you can walk on water is when it is frozen, remember, you can still suffer a slip and fall.*

So if the average board releases superintendents on their subjective feelings, and in their opinion you have not performed at the highest level of competence on the goals and objectives they created, using the evaluation instrument of their choosing, they will *terminate* you.

TERMINATION FOR CAUSE PROTECTION

We need some protection and to reduce the reasons for "cause" termination. These terms are better than the standard contract offering.

a. Termination for cause takes a *super-majority vote* of the board. On a five member board, it would take four board members to vote for termination.

   Why? If at the next board member election a new majority of board members are elected, that is the first sign a board will terminate the superintendent. Having that extra vote slows the new majority so they have time to get to know your strengths. This protects you from impulsive termination by new board members.

b. Termination for a cause of *malfeasance*, defined as dishonesty, illegality, knowingly exceeding authority for improper reasons. This is a much higher standard for termination.

c. There is also termination through the use of *binding arbitration to terminate the superintendent.* The board has an independent third party review their cause for action, and renders a decision that is binding on the board and superintendent. This keeps board opinion out of the process.

Point: A board should not be able to arbitrarily and capriciously terminate for cause based on their "feelings." They *can* terminate without cause and buy you out without any reason, and they should avail themselves of this board protection.

Case in Point: If the board sets your objectives and decides how to evaluate you without any input from the superintendent, you could end up with the following objective: *All students will be at or above grade level as measured by state tests.* When the results come in and you have not performed at the highest level of competence, as all students are not "at or above grade level," a rogue board member will push for your termination—breach of contract. *The devil is in the details of your contract language.*

TERMINATION TERMINOLOGY DEFINED

FOR "CAUSE"

Work is being done incorrectly, and it is negatively affecting the district in a material way, in the board's opinion. There is a lot of work that can be done incorrectly in the mind of a rogue board member!

When you are terminated for "cause" you receive no severance pay or benefits. You are done. You may be escorted to your office to clean out your personal belongings; turn in your keys. If you have a district vehicle, they will tell you to take a cab home. THAT'S IT.

PREFERRED LANGUAGE FOR TERMINATION FOR CAUSE

This requires a super-majority vote of the board at a regularly scheduled board meeting citing a "just cause reason of malfeasance." *Termination for a just cause of malfeasance is difficult for a board to prove.* A superintendent must do something very egregious and/or flagrant to be dismissed for just cause, such as taking bribes, illegal acts, hiring without board approval, etc.

TERMINATION "WITHOUT CAUSE"

This is a no-fault clause. The board has determined they want a different leader and therefore will pay you to go away without any reason or finding of fault.

The usual language will state "....the District shall pay *up to* x *months.*" Some boards will push for a four month to six month *"buyout"* provision. Hold firm for the maximum allowed by law. To secure another superintendent's position takes longer than four months to six months.

PREFERRED LANGUAGE FOR TERMINATION WITHOUT CAUSE

Never accept language that states the Board shall pay "UP TO x months." This means they will start negotiating your buy out at the <u>minimum</u>– you leaving immediately with <u>no</u> buyout payment, forcing you to settle somewhere below the maximum allowed by law.

Preferred terms will require a super-majority vote of the board at a regularly scheduled board meeting. The District shall pay "x months" with medical benefits, whether or not the superintendent finds employment within this period. Sometimes boards will have language that states if you secure employment within the buyout period they stop paying the buyout.

THANKS, BUT NO THANKS

No way! When they buy you out, it means *x* months, whether or not you find another position. Remember, when *x* months end, and you do not have employment, they won't ask how they can help. They have harmed you by letting you go, and they owe you X full month's pay and medical benefits. You may have had to relocate and uproot your family. That in itself is a major disruption to your life. Let them know this is *UNACCEPTABLE.*

If the Board has their attorney or search consultant negotiate with you, please remember-they represent the board, not you.

Contract language is important. Protect yourself and your family at all times! Remember this is a business deal not a date. *Stay focused and stay under control.* Every time I hear a new superintendent inform me that the board's attorney or search

consultant negotiated a good deal for them, I know one thing: *The superintendent did not get their best deal.*

> *The average board releases superintendents on their feelings, not on their performance (Andersen & Grissom, 2012).*

A superintendent phoned to tell me how great his new district was and that it practically ran itself. Two weeks later, he called to inform me the board terminated him without cause and bought him out at the end of his first year in the district. He was at a total loss of why it happened. This is why you want to secure a super-majority vote of the board to buy you out. Having the extra vote may keep you on the job. The next superintendent was let go a year later. Sometimes it is just a rogue board.

Critical point: This is politics, so it's, "I like you...I don't like you...don't confuse my opinion with your facts!" You want as much protection as you can negotiate.

KEY EVALUATION LANGUAGE

To be most effective, it is best to align all management evaluations to the same criteria as listed here. You want the management team to be accountable to achieve the same results you are to achieve, with the same professional behaviors you are held to.

For example: If you are accountable for improving test scores, you want to make certain your curriculum and instruction person has the same objective.

Key evaluation language needs to be annually and mutually agreed upon:

♦ objectives/ results

♦ duties/ responsibilities

♦ professional behavior

FIVE AREAS TO COVER IN THE CONTRACT

The following headings on evaluation were created by Dr. Kegham Tashjian of the San Bernardino County Superintendent of Schools Office. They form the basis for an all-inclusive evaluation system.

1 BOARD DIRECTION

"Mutually" agreeable objectives. A separate board-superintendent workshop every year to establish very clear and very specific objectives to measure your performance.

A satisfactory evaluation occurs when a majority of the board rates your performance as satisfactory. It is *their opinion.* Do not get in the trap of having to meet *a percentage of objectives*, say 7 out of 10, to be satisfactory, or a numerical rating, usually a 1-5 scale.

Let me explain: if you trap yourself into having to meet a percentage of overall objectives, you run the risk of watering down the objectives. You don't want to see a headline in the press stating *"Superintendent earns "F" for job performance"* if you only met 5 of the 10 objectives. You get the picture. If it is a slow news day, you will be in for a terrible time.

You want to push the envelope on your district results, as opposed to proposing objectives you know you will meet. For example, an objective that states "All students will be given the opportunity to take the state exam." Anyone can meet this objective. Compare that with "90% of students will meet or exceed state standards." Depending on the district, this could be extremely difficult to achieve.

The difference is that a percentage of objectives completed will force the superintendent to lower the standards for success over time, as rogue board members will attempt to score political points on your shortcomings by reporting it to the press. When their election comes around, they will throw you under the bus.

A satisfactory evaluation should never include an *average of numerical scores.* For example, if each board member rated the superintendent on a scale of 1-5 and then the scores were averaged for an overall rating, this allows one rogue board member to skew the scores. If four members rated the superintendent a 5 , and the fifth board member rated the superintendent a 1, the average would be 4.2, or 4/5.

A full board must vote on a satisfactory evaluation representing the majority of the board. It *should not* reflect a numerical score or percentage of objectives achieved, but simply a vote of the full board on whether they feel the superintendent performed satisfactorily.

2 BOARD SELF-EVALUATION

A board self-evaluation is needed prior to their evaluating the superintendent, so that their issues do not bleed over into your evaluation.

♦ Key point: the board cannot rate *themselves* "satisfactory" unless the superintendent is rated as satisfactory.

♦ It is a board-superintendent team. For one to succeed means all succeed, and vice versa.

3 SUPERINTENDENT

Board meetings <u>without you present</u> to discuss your evaluation are a DEAL BREAKER.

The superintendent is part of any meeting by the board to discuss the evaluation. You need to be able to know of the individual issues of each board member to be most effective.

4 INFORMAL MONITORING

Every three or four months, have a monitoring meeting during closed session with the board, for you to review your progress on achieving the mutually agreeable objectives.

At this time you want to include any limiting factors in the achievement of the objectives. For example, prolonged contract negotiations and a work slow-down may negatively impact test scores. This keeps the board informed about issues that you have to work through.

 # 5 THIRD PARTY FACILITATED

Have a third party present for each of these areas, to be able to question the board for understanding.

Close Call: A superintendent did not seek advice in drafting his contract, and the evaluation language was very fuzzy. The board took advantage of the fuzzy evaluation language and created new criteria based on an individual board member's problem with the superintendent. The superintendent saw the writing on the wall, and fortunately secured another position as an assistant superintendent in another district with a higher salary. He landed on his feet.

ROLE CLARITY

AUTHORITY

A well written contract clearly defines superintendent authority to avoid role confusion. *Role confusion leads to communication issues between the board and superintendent resulting in conflict and possible termination.*

As superintendent you are the CEO of the district. "The CEO is the highest ranking executive in a company, whose main responsibilities include developing and implementing high-level strategies, making major corporate decisions, managing the overall operations and resources of a company, and acting as the main point of communication between the board of directors and the corporate operations."(www.investopedia.com)

BOARD-SUPERINTENDENT ROLES AND RESPONSIBILITIES

To become a high performing board-superintendent team, roles need clarification and parameters defined for the professional working relationship to be effective.

SAMPLE LANGUAGE

Superintendent Duties: The Superintendent's primary responsibility is to manage the District to implement the *policy direction* of the board. The Superintendent shall be governed by and perform duties and responsibilities set forth in the laws of the state, formal duties as defined within this contract and by rules, regulations, and policies of the board.

The board shall not direct the superintendent to take any action that violates the terms and conditions of this contract.

The Superintendent:

a. Shall not act on individual board member direction, as this is a violation of the contract and grounds for termination of employment.

The above is good language to prevent a rogue board member from constantly meeting with you to get you to do something for them, like promoting or hiring a good friend.

b. Shall create a plan that assigns personnel and resources to achieve the board's policy direction. To include the organization or reorganization of the administrative and management staff to best serve the district. Shall have the *final authority* to *transfer or demote existing personnel*. Shall have the final authority to place principals at their schools.

c. Shall manage the day to day decisions of the district, to institute reforms and systemic changes as the superintendent finds necessary in order to affect positive changes in the district.

d. Shall administer all programs; funds; personnel; facilities; contracts; and all other administrative and academic functions subject to *oversight* of the board. (Oversight: suggestions or counsel by the board to the superintendent.)

e. Shall recommend all new employees to the District, or employees new to their position, to the board for their approval. The board reserves the right to accept or reject the Superintendent's recommendation to hire new personnel.

If the board rejects the Superintendent's final recommendation the Superintendent has the authority to make a new recommendation until it meets with board approval.

f. Shall attend all board meetings, closed and open sessions (including closed session to evaluate the performance of the Superintendent or to terminate the superintendent), study sessions, ad hoc meetings of board members and all board committee meetings.

Note: Have an annual board-superintendent workshop to review the contract. This is not to negotiate the contract but to review for understanding. This will also serve to help you understand individual Board member issues with your contract. Critical Point: just because one board member has a huge issue with some part of your contract do not consider changing your contract. It takes a majority vote to approve a contract. Don't be railroaded by one maverick board member and don't allow one board member to bully you into submission.

FINANCIAL SECURITY

You want a financial package that will be able to support you when you are let go. You need to get your mind right with this thought, otherwise you may leave your family at financial risk. They depend on you, so protect them at all times.

Remember, you are asking the board to contribute to your financial success, as you are the most vulnerable person in the district and most exposed to termination. You require financial protection to lead with confidence.

♦ Competitive Salary

♦ Tax Sheltered Annuities 403b

♦ Whole Life Insurance

a. **Competitive Salary:** Negotiate as strongly as you can, because you will not be able to negotiate any stronger in the future. Most superintendents give money away in the first year, and they will never be able to make up over time.

- If the board used a search firm they have done a salary analysis and that serves to help you set a salary. Remember, the search firm represents the *board,* not you.

- Check similar size district superintendent salaries to ascertain if this board is in the ball park.

You want contract language to represent a % number as opposed to a fixed amount. The % will go up automatically as your salary goes up. With a fixed amount, you will have to negotiate that separately.

b. **Tax Sheltered Accounts:** Negotiate with the district to pay a percentage of your salary, 1%-5% to start.

403(b) Tax Sheltered Accounts: Remember the rule of thumb: start small and work up over time.

c. **Whole Life Insurance:** You can compare whole life insurance and term insurance to owning a house versus renting one. Whole life has several features that are similar to owning a home: The premium (price) is fixed at the time of purchase. It accumulates cash value while you own it. The cash value increases over time. You can borrow against the cash value of the policy, and in certain ways this is like the ability to borrow against the equity in a home (Montgomery, 2016). In contrast, term insurance is like renting a home. You achieve no equity.

Whole life insurance provides savings for your use during your career as well as a death benefit. Ask the board to pay the premium or a part of the premium. If terminated you would be wise to use the cash accrued to sustain your expenses, as it is not taxed upon withdrawal. This is safe emergency money.

An excellent resource is AASA 2017-2018 Superintendent Salary Benefit Study authored by Finnan & McCord, 2018. Included in the study are numerous examples of Creative Contract Provisions submitted by superintendents.

Solution: *Stop being sold and start being informed.* A good start is Dave Ramsey's book, *The Total Money Makeover.* Next, invite different financial planners to your office with the admonition that you are looking to improve your employment contract with the board and would like some investment ideas to include in your contract proposal. Let them know you are seeking information only. They will oftentimes have contract language you can present to the board. If you include some investment ideas from a financial planner, be certain to have your district legal counsel review and approve prior to having the board act on your contract.

Make personal financial planning a regular part of your annual plan. Most superintendents I have worked with dislike being sold by financial planners or life insurance agents.

YOU ARE NOT A TEACHER—THINK LIKE A CEO

Superintendents tend to think like a teacher, with a relatively safe job where they will be employed for 35 plus years, deciding to retire when they want to. It doesn't happen this way for the average superintendent, and the superintendent needs to tuck away a large amount of money to prepare for unemployed down times.

The most effective superintendents have no financial worries, and they will out-perform superintendents living paycheck to paycheck. They have less to distract them from the duties of their job.

If you don't take care of yourself, why should anyone follow your leadership? In a discussion with a group of superintendents, we discovered two of the superintendents were the same age. One of them stated he had been a superintendent in several states and was not vested to retire in any one of them. On top of that he still had a teenage daughter living at home. Another superintendent said he too had been a superintendent in several states, and was vested to retire in all of them. I asked him if he had planned that, and he said, "Yes."

"Vested" means the number of years you need to be in education within a state to be eligible to receive retirement benefits. On average, states require from 5 to 10 years to vest. A few require fewer years of service. If you want to work in other states, it would be prudent to know this information. If you leave a superintendent's position after 8 years in a state requiring 10 years to earn retirement to accept a position in another state, you have just thrown away 8 years of your work life.

Why would anyone want to follow the leadership of someone who doesn't take care of their future, yet they are in charge of yours? People like to work for successful people. This is why it is more difficult to secure a superintendent's position after the board buys out your contract. The staff at the new district will quickly learn about the buyout and figure you are damaged goods. You will have a legitimacy problem to overcome with the new staff members.

FAILING TO HAVE A ROBUST FINANCIAL PACKAGE

A young, married, new superintendent with three children was informed the board was going to buy him out, and offered him six month's pay and benefits. He informed the board president that his contract stated he had a 12 month buy out provision. The board president informed him he was going to have to pay for an attorney to fight their action, as well as take them to court, and by the board's estimation he would end up with six months of buy out pay. He accepted their offer. When I asked him why he didn't fight this nonsense he said he couldn't afford to, as he didn't have the financial war chest. His situation didn't turn out so well and let's look at one that did turn out well as a result of contract language.

AN EXAMPLE OF AN EFFECTIVE COMPREHENSIVE CONTRACT

A superintendent was getting ready to begin his new job when a medical check-up put a hiccup in his plans. The doctor instructed him that he was not to report to work until he cleared him. The new superintendent informed the board president, and the board president became irate and stated, "We expect you to be on the job, or else."

The new superintendent took the doctor's advice and did not report to work. The board voted to dismiss the superintendent. The superintendent contacted his state administrative association and after a careful review of his contract, they paid for his legal defense against the board.

AN AIRTIGHT COMPREHENSIVE CONTRACT

Prior to signing his contract he sought advice from legal counsel, and it paid dividends. His contract clearly defined the terms and conditions for termination, and the board had violated his contract. He received a generous settlement. The humorous part is that he offered to be bought out for much less and the board said "No"— thought they were right. They learned they were wrong.

Attorneys that represent boards will tend not to want to represent you. The reason is that they work for boards and if they were known to work to represent superintendents the boards would no longer want to work with them. Your best bet is to contact your state administrative association for legal reference and contract review.

This situation could have turned ugly for the superintendent, but because he did his due diligence, practiced patience before signing off on his contract, his contract served to protect him. He *danced with the bear,* got a little bloody, but landed on his feet and is doing extremely well.

ADVANCED SALARY AND BENEFIT IDEAS

The following ideas are primarily for experienced superintendents seeking to re-negotiate their current contract or for those superintendents who are looking for a new superintendent position. The difference from a beginning superintendent is they have the experience and accomplishment "capital" to negotiate better terms and conditions of employment.

I would like to repeat my admonition that a superintendent is not a teacher, so we need to get out of the teacher mentality trap and start to think and behave as a CEO. My point is not to diminish the role of the teacher, but to point out the difference. Teachers negotiate as a group for the benefit of the group and thus negotiate for the average. If they negotiated as individuals, some teachers would earn more and receive more benefits than others. Some teachers would have more value within the organization. The union mantra is that all teachers are the same, and they negotiate as one, using peer pressure to effectively create solidarity. Superintendents are primarily former teachers and still have this mental trap to deal with to become a legitimate CEO and not a confused teacher. Peer pressure is effective at molding predictable behavior. We spend much time and effort assisting students to overcome peer pressure, and yet it seems a byproduct of our professional culture.

ADVANCED CONTRACT IDEAS

Advice: Whenever you are meeting with other superintendents and have the opportunity, ask if anyone has something in their contract they are happy to have included. This information will be invaluable to your contract.

Overtime: The superintendent may be compensated for up to 10 hours of paid overtime per week. Any time above 50 hours per week shall be considered overtime and paid at the rate of time and a half per the negotiated superintendent hourly rate of pay. The formula for hourly rate is total base salary divided by days in the work year divided by 8 hours.

Long Term Care Insurance

Disability Insurance

Life Insurance with paid premium in retirement

Doctoral Degree Reimbursement/ Education Fund: The district shall reimburse the superintendent for the tuition costs to earn an Ed. D. or Ph.D. from an accredited institution. The reimbursement shall be received at the conclusion of the program and only after the superintendent has been awarded the degree. The district shall annually budget an amount equal to the tuition costs of the institution. The board must approve the institution.

Investment Advice: With a satisfactory evaluation the board shall create a superintendent investment account of $5000 per each year of the contract. The amount shall accrue and if the superintendent has not used all or part upon leaving or retiring from the district the remaining amount shall revert to the district.

Health Maintenance Benefit: The superintendent shall receive $5000 per year if he/she is rated fit for duty by an annual physician exam.

Binding Arbitration: If the board moves to terminate the superintendent for cause the board and superintendent agree to have an independent third party hear the case and have binding authority on the superintendent and the board as to the decision. The third party shall be mutually agreed by the board and superintendent.

Super-majority vote required for termination for cause or without cause

District to Repay Student Loans: The amount shall be the minimum repayment amount as long as the superintendent is employed by the district.

District to Provide Personal Security if superintendent is in danger. The determination shall be made by the local law enforcement agency.

Medical/ Dental/ Vision Insurance: paid for the life of self and spouse in retirement

Post Retirement 403(b) Contribution: The district shall provide the Superintendent with a non-elective employer 403(b) retirement contribution equal to the statutory limit provided under §IRC 415c annual additions limit. Such contribution shall be 100% vested at all times. The contributions shall be made each year for five (5) calendar years following the year in which the Superintendent retires.

Retirement Audit: The district shall fully indemnify and provide mutually agreeable legal defense in the event the state audits the superintendent's employment contract or retirement income. In no case will individual board members be considered personally liable for indemnifying the superintendent against such demands, claims, suits, actions and legal proceedings.

❋ You can receive this fully paid by the district or negotiate to use your accrued vacation or sick leave-. Make certain you review this with a financial planner and legal counsel as it may need a Board policy.

Legal Defense Fund: If the superintendent receives a satisfactory evaluation the board shall contribute $10,000 per year for the life of the contract for a legal defense fund. The superintendent may use any portion of or the entire amount in the fund to provide legal defense not covered by the district, or to cover personal legal costs in the event the board moves to terminate the superintendent for cause. Upon leaving or retiring, the remaining amount shall be returned to the district.

CHAPTER 5

CONTRACT NEGOTIATING CYCLE

Dusting off your contract every 3 to 4 years to re-negotiate is a recipe for failure.

A. DRAFT YOUR CONTRACT

I read an article in the *San Diego Union Tribune* newspaper when a well- respected superintendent retired from a district. His quote stuck with me, *"They vetted my accomplishments, not my style."* In short, it wasn't a fit. His style was collaborative, and the board wanted top-down leadership. Being a highly successful experienced superintendent, he knew this and was of age to retire and did so.

WHAT FLOATS YOUR BOAT?

Time to consider what it will take for you to successfully lead a district. Think of your contract as a boat in rough seas – what will keep your boat afloat?

♦ What can the board do to help you do your best work?

♦ What can a board do to make you ineffective?

Time to take stock of your leadership style as well as your wants and needs as a superintendent. As an employee you took direction very well and turned it into a successful career. Now as a leader you will be giving direction.

It is wise to know your authority so that you and the board don't get involved in frustrating disagreements over role confusion. It is best if employees have one boss. They don't need mixed messages.

HOW COULD A ROGUE BOARD MEMBER CAUSE CHAOS?

"Boards that try to manage often end up generating unintended consequences. They undermine the CEO's credibility and authority to the detriment of the organization as a whole"

(Bader & Associates, 2008).

How might a rogue board member cause other board members to question your leadership? The contract needs to be clear – very clear – and sometimes that isn't enough.

A new superintendent with no experience working with boards ran into a rogue board member who constantly questioned her, berated her, and in her opinion, verbally harassed her. In short, he got into her head and under her skin. Her contract was airtight, but she couldn't shake her negative feelings and she asked to be bought out. She just wanted out in the worst way. We thought she was perfect for the job and the community, but a rogue board member got to her, and you know the rest of the story. At the next election he was voted out of office, but by then she was gone.

B. PRE-NEGOTIATIONS MEMO

♦ Serves to clarify for the board the areas of the contract that are most important to you, and why they are important

♦ It also serves to personalize you to the board

You want to bring into focus the importance of why you are asking for the items within the contract. Sometimes the board will not appreciate that you have a family. You would like for them to realize that you have greater interests than just serving their needs and impulses—you have a family that depends on you and you would like for them to understand this fact.

A board does not review contracts on a regular basis, and they are about as much fun for the board to review as it is for you to review. The pre-negotiations memo puts into focus your priorities in an easily understandable format—*a memo.*

♦ Attach the pre-negotiations memo to your contract and provide individual copies to each board member

♦ Discuss the memo with the board president or search consultant

For each applicant, the needs may be different. The average applicant will need:

♦ Job security

♦ Financial stability

♦ Role clarity

The employment contract requires you to carefully think through what is most important for your individual situation. You need to balance your lifestyle and leadership style.

SAMPLE PRE-NEGOTIATIONS MEMO

To: Board of Trustees

From: Superintendent Candidate

Subject: Contract Interests

I'm seeking a long term relationship with the district and to achieve this I have three primary interests I am asking the board to consider:

♦ **First Interest: Financial security for my family.** I desire a competitive salary, life insurance and tax shelter annuity that will provide me with the peace of mind to focus 100% on leading the district.

   • Reasons for these requests:

      ◦ The position of superintendent is the most vulnerable position and has the highest turnover rate in education, making it a financially insecure proposition.

      ◦ Financial security is important to me, as I have a family that depends on my income.

♦ **Second Interest: Clearly defined board and superintendent roles**

   • Reasons for this request:

      ◦ The major cause of Superintendent turnover is a dysfunctional relationship with the board caused by communication issues regarding role confusion.

- ○ High performing boards have a clear line of separation of responsibilities between the board and superintendent, sharing complimentary yet separate roles.

♦ **Third Interest: Reasonable job security.** As a new superintendent I will make mistakes, and I do not want the board to have a "hair trigger" response and move directly for termination.

- • Reason for this request:

    - ○ To provide job security so that the board doesn't move directly from mistake to termination.

C. NEGOTIATE CONTRACT

The devil is in the details. My advice is you can never put too much written detail into the contract, as it will serve as your cornerstone for being able to lead a successful district. *Your contract will enable your leadership or disable your leadership.* "A win-lose strategy of negotiations can damage future cooperation among group members as it undermines trust, inhibits dialogue and communication. Co-operative relations between negotiators are more effective if their power is equal (Deutsch, 1973).

The superintendent is in low power position during negotiations. Walton (1987) notes that "When power is unequally distributed the low-power person will automatically distrust the high-power person because he or she knows that those with power have a tendency to use it for their own interests" (Johnson, D., & Johnson, F,. 2000). The contract is your attempt to balance the playing field to build a foundation of board-superintendent trust.

NEGOTIATING THOUGHTS

"By failing to prepare you are preparing to fail."

~Benjamin Franklin

YOUR CONTRACT IS YOUR LEADERSHIP LESSON PLAN

You wouldn't want a teacher to start class without a quality lesson plan, and you should expect the same of yourself. Your contract will either assist or constrict your ability to lead. Your skill and knowledge will lead the district to further success, financially and academically. It's time to invest in yourself by getting your contract in order.

You are important. There will come a time you will want to retire or be forced into retirement. When that time comes you need to be financially prepared, or you will be forced to work past your expiration date, or be simply let go prior to being of age to retire. If you want to keep working that is different. If the work is still rewarding that's great. But if the day comes when you "hit the wall" or your health is being impaired, you need to be prepared to retire. This is the work of effective leaders—always be prepared.

When negotiating it is wise to keep in the back of your mind the Chinese proverb: "He who cares least wins most." What exactly does this proverb mean in terms of negotiating a contract? *Don't get emotionally attached to your contract proposal and emotionally hijacked during negotiations!*

When you negotiate a contract with a search consultant or attorney representing the board, or with board members themselves, you want to personally detach from the situation in order to keep your emotions in check. You don't want to be emotionally hijacked by personal attacks or laughter at one of your requests. No matter what is thrown your way, you want to picture a Teflon shield protecting you from insults and humiliation.

ROOKIE NEGOTIATING MISTAKE

It doesn't matter if this is your first contract or a successor contract. You need to own your contract. Let me explain. If a board member is concerned with your requests and asks, *"Where did you get this contract information?"* the professional response would be: "This is information I have gathered that I believe is most important for me to be successful in leading this district." *Own it!*

An anemic response would be, "Oh, I got this from so and so." This is called throwing someone under the bus. This is done often in administration office politics to keep you from being the central figure in a problem situation. *Own it.* This is *YOUR* contract proposal.

If you don't own it, don't present it. Yes, you have sought information from others as you did your due diligence, but this is your proposal. *This will gain you respect from board members.* Throwing someone under the bus will not earn you board member respect because you haven't demonstrated ownership of your position. You have demonstrated weakness in leadership decision-making.

Hopefully I have your attention on the importance of a well written employment contract. I could fill a book with the ugly superintendent stories of dirty deeds done by boards. When speaking with boards, they feel the same way. They could write a book of incompetent superintendent stories that damaged their district as well as their community. The problem with the board's side of the argument is that they hire the superintendent, so I would advise them to re-evaluate their hiring process and in particular the interview process. They need to ask what they could improve to get a better result.

"Never let the board feel they own you."

~Don Nielsen, 2015

Don Nielsen is the former Board President of Seattle Public Schools and a part time neighbor of mine. I asked him for advice for superintendents and he stated, "Never let the board feel they own you."

He went on to explain. "I think it is important for a superintendent to operate independent of board control and that can only happen if the board knows you don't need the job. The board's role is policy, not operations. Superintendents need to insist on this, and they can't do that if the board knows you need the job."

Some boards seem to prefer a contract that gives them maximum authority and control over the superintendent. They either want to own you through a bare bones financial package or control you with language stating you need board approval prior to making decisions. Always present in the back of their mind are all the stories they have heard from other boards about incompetent superintendent hires, and they want to protect themselves against failure. The responsibility starts and ends with the board.

Remember that most board members have never been in charge of a company, nor have they been a school superintendent. Most have not answered to a board, or even been a boss. This causes their own role confusion as to what exactly a board member has the authority to do.

Don Nielsen did not have this problem, as he had been a successful President and CEO of Hazleton Corporation. He knew how to run a profitable business. He understood the bottom line results, and after speaking with him my opinion is he would be the kind of board member who would give clear direction and wide latitude to perform on the job. His book, *Every School,* (2014) is an excellent read for superintendents and school board members to focus on district direction.

Finally, when a school board attorney speaks, boards tend to listen. Attorneys are paid to give boards as much latitude and power as possible. In short, when you are first hired, they will trust the attorney over you. This is why you need to be at the top of your game to secure a modicum of protection and flexibility to allow you to do the job as a partner within the board-superintendent team.

D. APPROVE NEW CONTRACT

When you receive an agreed-to contract, the job is not done. *A sincere thank you would be a good idea.*

♦ Send a personal note to the home of each board member to thank them for your contract and tell them you appreciate their willingness to negotiate with you.

♦ Apologize for any inconvenience you caused them, as this was not your intent; you were interested in creating a strong board- superintendent team.

♦ Tailor the message to fit the situation: If the negotiations went smoothly, simply thank them for the contract and tell them how much you appreciate their efforts to work with you.

E. MEDIA MESSAGE

If the media asks about your contract, a good response would look like this:

Stay on message: *"I appreciate the confidence the board has in my ability to lead the district!"*

Always say:

"I look forward to collaborating with outstanding educators."

"My goal is to prepare students to be successful in life."

Never say:

"I will fire ineffective staff members."

"The staff is overpaid."

Staff tends to remember negative messages, and the media loves the headlines.

PREPARE A BOARD PRESIDENT STATEMENT FOR THE NEW SUPERINTENDENT:

"As a board we are pleased the superintendent has accepted this outstanding contract offer. We selected this superintendent because of previous successful experiences."

♦ Improving student achievement

♦ Developing positive staff relations

Note: See Appendix A, School Board Media Message

You want the board to be able to state why they hired you. Practice the "broken record technique." Be prepared for the media to interview you with a barrage of questions. If there has been an issue with superintendent pay you need to have a media message, and practice the broken record technique of repeating it until the news reporter gets over it. We are not used to this, and it will take practice.

It goes something like this:

Reporter: *"How do you respond to those who feel your salary is out of line?"*

Superintendent: *"I appreciate the board's confidence in my ability to lead the district."*

Reporter: *"You are making more than the Governor. Is that fair?"*

Superintendent: *"I appreciate the board's confidence in my ability to lead the district."*

You get the idea. This is difficult, as we have never been in the world of politics. Remind yourself that you are in the world of politics, and must protect yourself at all times.

F. CELEBRATE SUCCESS

ACKNOWLEDGE AREAS NEEDING IMPROVEMENT

You are 100% responsible and accountable for everything in your district. Oftentimes you will not receive credit for what is working, but you will be held accountable for what failed. During times of trouble you may discover the myth of the management team — there is no team at all; you are on your own. Protect yourself at all times.

PROMOTING DISTRICT ACCOMPLISHMENTS

How is a board able to make the connection between district accomplishments and superintendent leadership, without personally establishing the link?

1. Every 6 to 12 months have your management team brainstorm what they have accomplished.

2. The best time to do this is before your evaluation and before their election, so the board has up-to-date information on what is being done in the district.

3. Present the information to your board. (Rotate speakers.)

    • Assign two managers to develop a presentation. One presents, the other assists.

    • The assistant will present at the next Celebrating Success board meeting.

    • This is a staff development opportunity for the entire management team.

    • After the presentation, I suggest you do an *After Action Review* of what worked and what can be improved, with regards to the presentation.

4. Ideally, board members will add to the list to make them a part of the team.

5. The important issue is to establish a link between *YOUR* leadership and results. This connection does not occur easily or readily: The message from the presenter would go like this, "Under the board and superintendent's leadership we have accomplished the following…."

    • Without this link, some board members will believe talented people are doing great work despite you, and not because of you.

    • The same is true for naïve administrators, who may believe that because you have not personally directed and personally monitored their work, they have done great things on their own.

- You do not want board members or administrators ever saying, "I have no idea what the superintendent does!"

6. The process allows the entire team to acknowledge what has been done and a sense that they have a responsibility to accomplish something, rather than just manage day to day issues.

G. ANNUAL CONTRACT REVIEW

Annually, have a special board workshop to do two things:

♦ Review the superintendent employment agreement for understanding and clarification. (This is not a time to re-negotiate the contract).

♦ Conduct a board self-evaluation.

I preferred the first Saturday in February from 8:30- 11:30 am. Breakfast is provided. You want to make certain everyone understands what was agreed to. It is also a good time in case you have a new member elected in November. They would have attended a meeting in December and perhaps one or two in January. They would be ready to understand your contract.

I have known superintendents who refuse to do this, as it causes discussion and could promote issues that have been put to rest in the past. My opinion is—I want to know who has a problem.

Remain cool, calm and collected. When teaching a college course a student asked, "Do superintendents go through special training to not react to problems?" I explained the training is the *"school of hard knocks!"*

♦ It is *each court case* where you take the stand, knowing the attorney wants to show you made a mistake or committed a wrongdoing.

♦ It is *each board meeting* where a board member wants to question your intelligence or decision making ability.

♦ It is *each parent-packed board meeting* where they demand not to close a school or to change school boundaries.

♦ It is *each staff-packed board meeting* demanding their interests be met.

♦ It is *each community member* who accosts you in public about a decision they don't agree with.

It is special training, and it is very effective at shaping how you react—especially with social media ever present. You will either learn to listen and not react emotionally, or you will be *eaten by the bear*.

CHAPTER 6

POLITICS AND THE FIRST 24 MONTHS

"Any superintendent who says, this political stuff is not for me, accepts unnecessary limits to their ability to improve education and serve children."

~Paul Hill, 2018

POLITICS

I like you... or, I don't like you... or, What have you done for me lately? I have found school superintendents, as a rule, to be responsible, self-effacing professionals. They are truly decent people, responsible for leading multimillion dollar organizations. Collectively they form the backbone of the future of our nation, with an educational mission to prepare students to achieve the American dream. You have been successful as a teacher, school site administrator, principal, and district office administrator, and now superintendent of schools. We don't want you blindsided by the politics of the job.

BLINDSIDE #1

An assistant superintendent told me the story of when he became superintendent. He said he and the superintendent were in closed session with all five board members. Everything had been going well in the district and there were no surprises at the board meeting. Out of the blue, the board president asked the assistant superintendent if he wanted to be superintendent. He said he figured the board had just fired the superintendent, and that if he didn't accept the offer he might be fired next. So he said "Yes." I asked if he had ever spoken with the superintendent about this situation. He said, "No."

This is an example of why you always need to be prepared with your contract, ready to step up and lead.

I would have recommended he ask the obvious: Is the superintendent retiring? When caught off-guard you need to buy some time: "Yes, I would like to be superintendent, and I would like to see the contract before actually agreeing to the position."

BLINDSIDE #2

A board directed a superintendent in his first year to reassign a high school principal to the classroom on a 5-0 direction from the full board. The new superintendent formally notified the principal in March. By June the high school principal had rallied staff, students and parents to his cause and the board terminated the 1st year superintendent's contract on a 5-0 vote of the board. The principal remained the principal. The superintendent retired. This is politics!

Success is all you have known, and we want to keep it that way. Our strength, when used to excess, is also our weakness. We trust in the fact that we can work through any situation with the professional behavior that got us this far in our career.

UNFORTUNATELY NOT!

Superintendents are in the world of politics because their boss, the school board, is *elected.* Think in terms of "I like you... I don't like you." This is politics, and it is not always based on fact and professional thinking. Your contract is an attempt to define a professional working relationship with the board. It serves to protect you from impulsive termination because of board likes and dislikes.

For example, if at the next election a new majority of board members are elected, spearheaded by an individual that has a personal problem with you, what protection do you have from arbitrary termination?

Contract language to avoid: "Termination without cause." The Board can terminate the superintendent's employment contract with a simple majority vote of the Board and four month's severance pay. You want the maximum amount as the state law allows and a super-majority vote of the board to buy you out.

PAYBACK

A superintendent phoned me when this happened to her. A new majority was elected to her board. She stated the current board will have one more board meeting before the new board takes control, and they wanted to know if she would like for them to exercise their right to *terminate her without cause,* i.e, buy her out. She stated she had always been able to work with anyone and felt she could in this situation.

The situation arose because the superintendent had recommended an assistant superintendent for termination, and the board agreed. The assistant superintendent wanted payback for her dismissal and recruited a slate to run for the board. They were elected. It became public knowledge that the former assistant superintendent was out to get her. I informed her, that in my opinion, she should take the buyout and move on.

As an excellent superintendent, she contacted several other sources including her state administrative association, and decided to take the buyout. She is now doing extremely well at a private university. She was cool, calm and collected, weighed all her options, and didn't let reckless behavior dictate her decision. She made a thoughtful leadership decision and moved on.

In the book "The Art of War," Sun Tzu states one of his five leadership mistakes is to be <u>reckless</u>, which would cause someone in our situation to be fired. Because she had emotional balance as a leader, she survived a potentially devastating end to an excellent career. Imagine a new board majority harassing the superintendent with inflated charges of breach of contract. Think of the newspaper headlines—even if she survived the politics of this situation from that moment on, she would be forever tagged on social media. She made the right decision. As difficult as it was to make the decision, she made it.

DYSFUNCTIONAL BOARDS

In contracts there is usually a clause: *Termination Without Cause.* Simply stated, most contracts require a *majority vote* with no reason to buy you out, with "UP TO x months" of buyout payments. I asked an attorney who stated he had negotiated over a thousand superintendent contracts for school boards, "What in your opinion causes superintendent termination?" Without hesitation he exclaimed, *"Dysfunctional school boards."*

Items 8 & 9 in the Sample Contract (see Chapter 12) discuss termination. Ask the board for a super-majority vote of the board for Termination without cause and for termination with cause. <u>Super-majority</u> on a five member board is four. <u>Simple majority</u> would be three votes of a five member board. This extra vote may provide needed protection until you have had time to work through issues with the board that are normal and natural during the first 24 months.

THE AIRPLANE IS GOING DOWN

Airlane pre-flight instructions state that in the event of a problem the oxygen mask will come down, and you are to place it on your face before you assist anyone else. The reason is simple—if you are in distress, you are of no value to others.

Your contract is your oxygen mask. If you don't adjust it properly in the beginning, you will not be able to help others, as you will be in constant distress.

YOUR CONTRACT AND YOUR SUCCESS ARE LINKED

Successful superintendents understand the importance of their employment contract as it creates the conditions necessary to effectively lead a school district. Inexperienced or first time superintendents simply don't understand the connection. They are stepping into a political world where they have no direct experience or training. It is at this juncture most new superintendents will gain a new found appreciation of their former superintendent.

NO COMPARISON TO SURVIVING OFFICE POLITICS

Naïve superintendents think in terms of former administrators they worked with who played office politics. They attempted to make themselves more upwardly mobile by throwing others under the bus and participating in backstabbing, rumor mongering, and in general just being catty. You survived them by simply not getting in the mud with them. These superintendents trust the skills of responsibility, hard work and loyalty that propelled them to the pinnacle of educational success will keep them in good stead with the school board. *Politically savvy, they are not.*

As one superintendent search consultant said, "You can have a school board that has gone through nine superintendents in nine years, but you will always find a willing applicant who knows they can do the job no one else has been able to do. Then that same board, the following year, will have gone through ten superintendents in ten years."

POLITICS OF THE MANAGEMENT TEAM

A search consultant stated that he is always amazed when superintendents are upset when a management team member "sells them out" to the board. He said, "When there is a problem there is no team; superintendents are on their own." This is the reason you rely on the strength of your contract; you may be terminated because of the lack of specificity of your contract.

A new superintendent wanted to increase school site budgets and the principal's authority to make decisions. An assistant superintendent of curriculum and instruction didn't like this idea, as she had a pet project she wanted funded and the new organizational structure caused her loss of power to control how money was spent.

It took over a year for the superintendent to find out that the assistant superintendent went behind his back to inform principals that they must fund her special project or she would cut off their categorical funding. It took this long for one principal to muster the strength to let the superintendent know. Once the information came out, the superintendent informed the assistant superintendent that she had the rest of the year to locate a new position or she would be returned to the classroom the following school year.

It is best to have contract language that clearly states your authority to organize or reorganize the administrative and all management staff who, in your judgment, best serve the district. To assign principals to their schools and transfer or demote existing personnel. The superintendent is best served by developing a process to let the administrative team know of his/her authority. This is also the reason the superintendent would be wise to have an annual meeting with the board to review the contract to understand roles of each party.

He could do this on the strength of his contract giving him authority to lead, and because the board reviewed this prior to signing off on his contract. He explained to the board of his direction and collaborative style of leadership and the possible issues it would create, such as members of his team would lose power. He further explained he would need the board to back him if he demoted or transferred personnel in such situations. They agreed, which gave him confidence to follow through on his decision. The assistant superintendent left the district, and the principals got the message loud and clear that they were responsible to lead their schools.

Communication with the board is a must. Sometimes communicating is hard to do, but your leadership issues will get worse if you fail to communicate and work through issues together. The key is your poise under stress.

THE PROBLEM IS LOSS OF CONTROL

First time superintendents are thrown into a state of emotional upheaval as a result of losing control of their work environment. They quickly learn they are in a board environment of 24 hour "I heard…." board members will contact you with information that is third- and fourth-hand, and distorted by the agenda of the messenger.

Some superintendents dive right in and get to the bottom of the rumors, while others will be totally frustrated, as this is keeping them from their job. As a superintendent, it is wise to know if you are a collaborative leader or a top down leader. Do you prefer principals to have the authority and control of their budget to make leadership decisions, or do you prefer a central office giving direction to the principals? It is best to think through this basic issue in order to negotiate language into your contract that will complement your leadership style.

ALIGNMENT

We are continuously striving for alignment of our board and superintendent team, as well as for alignment of superintendent and management team. I'm addressing alignment on direction, objectives, values and style of leadership. You want to be able to send a message to your management team that, "We are heading north. If you want to go south, you need to consider a new team that will meet your needs."

You can only send a strong message if you have negotiated clear and strong language to give you the confidence to lead with a strong message. When I first became a superintendent my assistant superintendent for business was also our chief negotiator. During our first negotiations together he objected to how I wanted him to negotiate, as he was trained in adversarial bargaining and I wanted an open collaborative process. One day he met with me in private and stated, "I was trained that you cannot negotiate style." I countered, "Well we have negotiated in a bureaucratic style for years, so don't tell me we don't negotiate style."

We are always negotiating: with staff, community members, businesses, and every few years with the board on our contract. Negotiating takes practice, and remember you are always negotiating– stay ever-vigilant.

He came back at me by stating, "Then you need to find a new negotiator." My back at him comment, "I'll be glad to, but as your contract states that you are the negotiator for the district, I'll need to accept your resignation from this district." His facial features gave away that this thought had not occurred to him as he was well respected by the board. He also had a copy of my contract, and he was politically astute enough to have read it thoroughly, so he knew the authority the board had granted me.

I had a fixed look with a straight face. I was not mad or emotional. He knew I meant business—there was no mistaking it. After a lengthy pause I stated, "Now if you have a problem resigning from the district, I advise you to get the job done in the manner I have directed you to." As he turned to leave my office, B.F. Skinner rang through my mind. I said, "Look, I know this is hard for you, and I also know you are excellent at collaboration, and you will secure a good outcome." With this direction, he secured the first 3-year negotiating agreement for as long as anyone on the teachers' negotiating team could remember—a job well done. Strong clear direction comes from the confidence provided within the language of your contract.

Positive reinforcement moves people in the desired direction. Repeated negative reinforcement is a dumb tactic.

~B.F. Skinner

FUZZY CONTRACT LANGUAGE

A new superintendent was having a problem with the board interfering with personnel selections. Specifically, the board wanted the superintendent to bring to them the top three school principal candidates, for the board to select the finalist. The new superintendent argued that she was to advance the finalist to the board for approval.

I asked to see her contract, and found that there was no mention of the personnel selection process. The board could do as they pleased. The superintendent informed me that she discussed this at length with the board before she signed the contract, as this was a problem in their past. But if it is not in the contract, it doesn't exist. After a year of feeling out of control, she left the district.

Negotiate into your contract that you will be allowed 5 days of mentoring, usually provided by the search firm during your first year, and an optional 5 days during the second year. You will need to reach out and share your frustrations and success stories. Remember the job is lonely. See the mentoring clause in Chapter 12, #22.

A GREAT PLACE TO WORK

Years ago I read a book by Robert Levering, *A Great Place to Work* (1988), and as I recall, a characteristic of a great place to work was that the employee had control of their work environment. As a new superintendent you quickly realize you don't have control. It is as if you are in a sailboat without a mast, rudder, or centerboard during a storm. You are attempting to get your sea legs but with each new wave you are slammed to the deck.

It is best if you go into the job knowing you will be taken to task by one or more board members. The point is not that you keep getting knocked down; it is that you get back up that matters. It is the fact that a few board members will not be able to run you off. You are going to weather the storm. Being politically savvy is required. It is like that rookie teacher who keeps falling on their face with each lesson, but they don't quit until they find their balance. You will need to find your political balance, and the first requirement is to admit your job is political.

BALANCING ACT

In the beginning the job is literally 24 hours each day. You will be answering to board questions and concerns as well as assessing the district and evaluating administration. The time you take now to address concerns and look after your health will pay off when you get your systems in place.

CONTROLLING YOUR ENVIRONMENT

Those who can balance the politics of the job while leading a district have a chance to succeed. They have learned to manage their work environment. Those who don't, leave the position, and usually never want back in.

The basic problem is the fact that "The governance process causes role confusion by creating shared decision-making between the board and superintendent. The board is making operational decisions" (Dawson & Quinn, 2000). Get control of your environment via contract language that is clear and specific. *Your contract provides some measure of control of your work environment.*

ALWAYS NEGOTIATE WITH THE ROGUE BOARD MEMBER IN MIND

Every once in a while you run into a problem board member. They want power, or control, or they just like to stir the pot for their own enjoyment. It amazes me, with all the great people that become great board members, the public will elect the rogue candidate that causes problems for the superintendent, other board members, students, staff, and the community as a whole.

Imagine yourself and the board in a rowboat. It is difficult enough to have everyone rowing in the same direction with the same stroke rate. Just when everyone is going in the same direction, you have the rogue board member throwing an anchor over the side of the boat, making it come to a sudden stop. Everyone is thrown into a panic. These are the rogue board members. They are the reason you draft a comprehensive employment contract.

If you remember one thing from this book, remember this: *Failure to negotiate a comprehensive contract could result in your failure as a superintendent.* As is said in the boxing ring — protect yourself at all times.

> *"The fight is won or lost far away from witnesses — behind the lines, in the gym and out there on the road, long before I dance under those lights."*

~Muhammad Ali

Before the curtain goes up and you step under the lights and into the ring of public opinion to lead a school district, do your due diligence and draft a comprehensive contract that will provide you the opportunity to be an effective leader.

As Board members are elected there are those rogue board members who believe they only answer to the voters and will not abide by any rules imposed by other board members. As the CEO of the district, it is best if the superintendent brings in a third party facilitator to review effective board member behavior. The point is if a rogue board member does not want to be part of the board team then the other board members need a strategy to exclude that member until they learn to be a Team member and quit acting as a separate stand-alone board. (See the Team Protocols in Chapter 11.)

It is best to have this discussion when adopting the protocols. The question becomes, "What do we do if someone repeatedly violates the protocols?" I say "repeatedly," as everyone makes mistakes.

ONE EXAMPLE OF HOW TO HANDLE ROGUE BOARD MEMBER

What to do if a board member repeatedly violates the Protocols:

1. In *open session* the board president informs the rogue board member that their behavior is unacceptable.

2. If the behavior continues, the rest of the board will not respond to questions or concerns from this board member. The board president simply clarifies, "Is there anything else?"

3. No board member will second a motion by this board member.

4. The motion will fail because of a lack of a second. If it is a good motion, then another board member will make a new motion. Petty? Childish? No. Everyone must know their role and expected behavior to become a high performing team.

5. In point of fact the board will "shun" the rogue board member until he or she becomes a member of the board team.

Peer pressure is the best tool to shape behavior.

Almost no board will get to this point, but it is important for them to consider what they will do if a rogue board member gets out of control. They need their crisis plan.

CHAPTER 7

THE VALUE OF LEADERSHIP

No one factor makes a company admirable – but if you were forced to pick one that makes the most dramatic difference, you'd pick leadership.

(Bennis, 1999)

The position of superintendent has an unrivaled influence on education. The stability or longevity of the superintendent is twice as important as comprehensive school reform in improving student achievement (Waters & Marzano 2006). The importance of the superintendent can never be understated and in the words of life coach Ann Bruce, *"If we undervalue what we do, we undervalue who we are."*

At the opening of your contract negotiate to have the following belief statement: The purpose is to create an annual discussion topic between the board and superintendent on understanding respective roles.

BOARD-SUPERINTENDENT BELIEF STATEMENT

"The board has one employee—the superintendent, and the board believes a high-performing board-superintendent team has the greatest impact on education because of the authority vested in these positions. Teamwork is not sharing decisions between the board and the superintendent; it is sharing complementary yet separate roles. The board knows the position of superintendent has the highest turnover rate in education, making it the most vulnerable position within the district. For these reasons, the board believes it is necessary to clearly define the duties of the superintendent and the board to serve as a basis for effective communication and teamwork in the management of the school district. By doing so, the board believes this will enhance superintendent stability, longevity and effectiveness, improving the overall quality of the educational program and the operational success of the district."

At this point you want to practice negotiating on working through "No" as some boards will refuse to allow this into the contract. Start with, "Why?" What is the board's concern?" You want to get them to talk and talk and talk to help them through their issue and to assist you in understanding their reasoning

The board wants you to recognize they are ultimately responsible, but they will hold you accountable.

By not paying close attention to the employment contract you are not valuing the position of superintendent. More importantly you are not protecting yourself or your family.

ALMOST SOLD OUT THE FAMILY

A new superintendent had a brush with ending his career. He failed to clearly define when his contract would be renewed and what happens if the deadline to renew is missed. The superintendent had very fuzzy language and got within a six month window until his contract terminated. Fortunately he secured an assistant superintendent position in the nick of time in another district. He was an excellent, trusting person, and this was a little too close for comfort.

Success starts with the superintendent contract. Successful superintendent leadership adds to a district's bottom line financially and academically. In 2003, I attended a meeting with Dr. Susan Scalafoni, then Assistant Secretary of the U.S Department of Education. She stated that, "Without a coherent district, learning for all will not occur."

Hope adds 12% in achievement (Shane Lopez, 2015).

It is the responsibility of the superintendent to add coherence to a district. Teachers have a need for stability within a district to perform at their best without distraction. Remarkable teachers are exceptionally focused on their students through the teaching and learning process. They depend on the superintendent's leadership to bring coherence to the district so they can remain focused on their students. Stability of leadership brings HOPE to staff. Leadership provides a future focus and a message of hope within systems that keep the organization fixated on quality.

85% Of problems are systems problems, not people issues (W. Edwards Deming).

This is why you want the term of your contract that is the maximum allowed by law in your state, as leader stability brings coherence to the district.

Steve Zuieback, organizational consultant stated, "The first stage of organizational decline is operational decline- Things just aren't working right." This starts with the superintendent contract. As superintendent you have a fiduciary responsibility to draft a comprehensive contract to provide the framework to produce a high performing system. Your contract serves as the foundation to build confidence in your leadership.

A high performing management system removes the barriers for teachers to teach at the highest levels of competence. They depend on your leadership even though they will not know why. The reason is simple: when things are working effectively, they believe this is the norm. When things aren't working right, the best performing teachers hunker down and wait for the superintendent to pass on to another district. Dysfunctional staff members will have a field day, perpetuating doubt throughout the collapsing system.

Jim Clifton, CEO of Gallup Organization, in his book *The Coming Jobs War* identifies dysfunctional employees as "actively disengaged" as they actively attempt to destroy the good work of the district. On average, 19% of employees are actively disengaged, which means that no matter how well things are working throughout the district, you have on average 19% looking to point out problems and issues. The leadership plan is to provide a voice to our productive employees and not let the actively disengaged workers control the message.

District coherence and operational effectiveness begins with the superintendent employment contract. The contract defines the professional working relationship and operational boundaries between the board and the superintendent. A well written contract defining the role of the board and superintendent is an important first step in creating organizational stability leading to success.

Selecting personnel is a potential problem area you want to clarify in the contract, as some board members want to select or promote friends. Contract language should clarify-this: the superintendent <u>selects</u> personnel and the board <u>approves</u> personnel.

For a school district to be successful, trust and honesty must exist between the superintendent and board (Plotts, 2011). Trust is built when positive values and results are achieved, as this allows staff and community to predict future behavior based on past behavior. Defining expected board and superintendent behavior is the building block to establishing a professional working relationship between the board and the superintendent to work as a team.

At an NSBA Conference in 2006, I had the pleasure to listen to Benjamin Canada from the Texas Association of School Boards. He said, *"Success at the top means success at the bottom."* The "top" is the board and superintendent team, as they have the legal authority to make decisions for the organization. Success and stability begins with the contract. Before you sign your name on the contract and before you have spent one minute on the job, take the necessary precautions to understand the ramifications of your contract. Read it from the viewpoint of *"What is the worst that could happen?"*

YOU COULD LOSE YOUR JOB IN THE NEXT TWO WEEKS

All superintendents have two weeks left on their contract. It doesn't matter if you have signed the maximum contract allowed by law; you can be terminated without cause at the next board meeting. (Board meetings are typically every two weeks.) A superintendent related how difficult the life of a superintendent is. He lamented that his board meetings are scheduled every two weeks and each meeting runs long and late into the night. He confided that he would return home after each board meeting and his wife would have a glass of wine waiting for him. He laughed, "I come in the door and say to my wife, 'Good news... we're staying another two weeks.'"

THE SWORD OF DAMOCLES

A superintendent sits with the sword of Damocles over his head. The quick version of the story: Damocles wanted to know what it was like to be king. His king, Dionysius, invited him to sit on his throne. As Damocles felt the power of the throne, the king had his sword tied by the single hair of a horse's tail above his head. Damocles said fearfully, "The sword could fall at any time and kill me!" Dionysius replied, "Now you know what it is like to be king."

We usually remind our students to have impulse control and to practice their patience. Before you sign an employment contract and jump into the chair of leadership, now is that time. You don't want your career hanging by a thread.

The employment contract is the weakest part of the superintendent's job preparation. Unfortunately, most new superintendents spend more time preparing for the job interview than preparing their contract. The same level of thought and preparation that you put into your interview needs to go into your employment contract. Your contract language will either facilitate a smooth road to working with the board, or will feel like they just ran you off the road and over a cliff.

I DIDN'T SEE THAT COMING

With a little more negotiating you can solve most of the communication problems and role confusion issues you will experience from a defectively written contract. It is worth your mental and physical health to do so.

So, before you start working on the work, work on your contract! You don't want to end your professional career because of a flawed contract that you at best only gloss over and don't understand; that's until the board exercises their right to terminate you without cause and buy you out!

You want the legal maximum contract and a super-majority vote of the Board to either dismiss you or to buy you out. If the board is adamant about not giving you the super-majority vote of the board ask for this for the first two years of the contract. You also want language that states the board cannot reassign you to any other position as you were hired as the superintendent. Why? You want longevity on the job to provide stability to the district.

A DIFFERENT SKILL SET IS NEEDED

Never trust you will be able to work through any issues with the board just as you have successfully negotiated professional issues throughout your career. As one superintendent confided, *"I would have taken the job without a contract."*

There is a euphoric feeling in being selected to the highest position of a district. You have arrived and your hard work, long hours of preparation has been recognized by the school board. Being a superintendent is a different game. It is politics at the lowest level. School boards are the closest politicians to the community and they will hold you personally accountable for what goes wrong. Literally everyone has access to them. As a new superintendent one phone call from a disgruntled parent or well respected staff member with a problem can start a chain reaction of questioning your decisions, to mistrust, ending in dismissal. Remember it is about "liking and/or not liking you."

The first 24 months on the job are critical as people are just getting to know you. Walking into the job, you usually won't have years of relationships built by working through issues with the board together as a team. You won't have the trust of your district administrators, principals, teachers or classified members.

Trust is built by working through problems over time, achieving results, and living values. Staff members do have some degree of trust with the individual board members as they may have taught their children and may have helped get them elected. You will be walking on thin ice for some time. One misstep and you will break through the ice, starting a cold downward spiral of helplessness and potentially ending your career.

SOCIAL MEDIA

Will Rogers said, *"You never get a second chance to make a good first impression."* Today with social media, the speed at which information flows is astounding.

You need to have every aspect of your game plan "ready from the jump."

♦ Media message

♦ Staff message

♦ Management direction

♦ Academic direction

♦ Financial direction

Where do you plan to lead the district and exactly how do you plan to get them there? *Loving students and valuing staff are not enough. Superintendents need a "toolbox" of skills to manage and lead a complex organization.*

SKILLED LEADERS REQUIRED

Social media is cruel and unforgiving. Those who recognize this "from the get go" will be more successful. Before you start your first day on the job, district staff will know all about you—warts and all. Remember, if you have had a problem, never try to *explain* your way out; instead *perform* your way out of a problem.

The contract serves to keep the board and superintendent future-focused with clear roles and objectives so that, together, both parties can perform their way out of any problem. *It allows the leadership of the board and superintendent to amplify their effectiveness.* I have heard more than one veteran superintendent lament that they wish they could go back and rewrite their original contract as roles were confused leading to avoidable problems.

SEEK ADVICE BEFORE SIGNING THE FIRST CONTRACT

Why is this? Well, in the beginning we were just so elated to get the job. We didn't feel special or deserving of a good contract, and the board members were so friendly and excited—how could anything go wrong?

LOOKS LIKE YOU'RE IN OVER YOUR HEAD

Imagine a board handcuffing a superintendent's hands and feet and then throwing the superintendent into the ocean a mile off-shore. They say, "Your goal this year is to swim to the beach." If that weren't bad enough, a storm is developing! This is how some contracts are written, in order to provide the board with maximum control. Next, the board states the obvious, "Looks like you're in over your head."

Power over, not power with (Tom Terez, 2010).

Most boards do not do this maliciously. They are concerned about a superintendent getting out of control, primarily with staff or finances. They want protection. They don't see that their controlling contract language impedes their district from being as successful as it could be by allowing the superintendent the freedom to lead. Many have never run an organization and don't understand what a CEO needs to successfully lead. They understand *control* and they have heard terrible superintendent stories from other boards. It is simply self-protection.

For a superintendent to manage successfully a board must govern effectively. School board attorneys do not want contract language that confines the board's ability to do what they want, when they want, and how they want. The attorney is not interested in the success of a superintendent. They are interested in keeping board authority in place. From the beginning this sets up possible conflict and role confusion. The new superintendent needs clarity of job roles to perform optimally, and the board is concerned about giving away too much power to someone they don't know, and being accused of being a "rubber stamp" board.

REDUCE VARIATION IN THE SYSTEM

When a contract is not carefully crafted to define the roles of the board and superintendent, the new superintendent will spend an inordinate amount of time trying to listen to and be attentive to several board member's wants, needs and wishes. This creates variation in the system, detracting from being a quality organization and this can take a toll on productivity.

To improve quality within an organization, it is necessary to reduce the variation within the system. The contract should focus the superintendent to reduce variation between board and superintendent roles.

Imagine a team of horses pulling in several different directions. If they were pulling in the same direction, they would go farther faster. This is the role of your contract.

> *Rookie superintendents don't understand the complexity of being the CEO. "Superintendents think like middle managers in the private sector, as they like to check off tasks completed as opposed to having a clear desk and thinking about where their district should go and how to get it there" (Dr. Clayton Lafferty, 1989).*

As we came up through the ranks of administration we always worked for a boss. We were the subordinate. As we enter the first superintendent's position, we readily assume the subordinate position to the board and as such follow their direction and *take the first contract the board offers without question.* We don't see ourselves as the CEO with a specific role to play, let alone consider negotiating our role with the board, as they are the boss. We see ourselves as taking direction from the board, checking off the tasks they assign as opposed to collaborating with the board on district direction. As time passes we get comfortable in the position, and we don't want to ask for anything out of the ordinary because there are always one or two board members who overreact to spending one more penny on your contract or giving you more authority to lead.

NEGOTIATING FOR YOURSELF IS VERY UNCOMFORTABLE

Let's try an easy scenario.

The board offers a three year contract and you ask for four years. They respond, "We never give four year contracts!"

What do you think you should do? Do you fold and say, "OK"? They are the boss and I don't want to upset them. No! Get back in there and ask, *"Why not?"* Most likely you will be working with a search consultant, who represents the board. The search consultant is probably a retired superintendent.

Pay maximum attention to the advice I am about to give: The search consultant wants you and the board to be happy. But remember, the search consultant represents the board. It is during this process that superintendent candidates become "chatty"—they over-share information to the search consultant about what they would accept. The search consultant will advise the board, based on this information, what "in his opinion" you will accept. It is like being in court on the witness stand—answer the questions directly, but don't explain and don't add detail.

I am not advising to be rude or unprofessional to the search consultant; you will want to forge a relationship with the search consultant for future superintendent positions. I'm advising you to *protect yourself at all times*. There is a difference between saying, "I would really like a four year contract but if the board is adamant I can live with three years." That is *very weak* as opposed to a strong position, "This is a problem for me, as I would like to send a message to the staff and community that the board fully supports me with a four year contract. I request you present this to the board again for their consideration."

As you say this, look the person in the eye and don't blink. Don't be angry; be positive—and don't blink. You are serious. It is at this juncture you will start to realize being the superintendent is a lonely job.

NO DOESN'T ALWAYS MEAN NO—BE PERSISTENT

If we don't counter the board's proposal and simply accept every "No" they state, we are responding from a weak position. As the British statesman Robert Walpole declared, *We are letting sleeping dogs lie.*

In the process we put ourself and our family at risk, by having to put out fires that wouldn't have been there if we had paid attention to our contract and stuck up for what we knew we needed to lead an organization. Jim Collins sums it up, "The enemy of being great is being good."

We don't want to risk going outside of our comfort zone. We don't want to ask for anything too different as this might upset the board. Furthermore, we have never been confrontational in our career and don't like this feeling. We have always been the go-to person to get the job done; no problems or complaints.

TIME TO LEAD

"If you don't stand for something you'll fall for anything."
~Alexander Hamilton

There is an assumed point in being a leader that I have made throughout this book, and I want to address it at this time. I have stated a leader needs a direction, a plan to achieve it and the basic values to drive his or her decision-making. The major issue that causes superintendents to accept the first contract offered by the board is that they do not have a direction or a plan, and haven't thought through their values to drive their decisions. They are accepting the position fully prepared to take the board's direction, as they have never considered where they would like to take education. In short, they will *manage* a district with direction from the board, as opposed to *leading* it into the future. It is very difficult to be strong at the negotiating table with a weak educational leadership foundation. *Always be prepared to step into your future.* What is your morally compelling purpose that drives you to want to lead others?

YOUR STORY WILL LEAD TO YOUR EDUCATIONAL PURPOSE

Let me explain my personal story, as best as I remember the facts of the situation. I had a friend in high school, Junior (not his real name) who died from a drug overdose. Prior to his death, his mother left a note stating that she was leaving to run off with her boyfriend. Junior was left to fend for himself. His father had died some time previously from alcoholism.

Junior was a fun loving, good guy, without a malicious bone in his body, and now was a time he could have used some adults to provide direction to his life. That didn't happen. I remember speaking with one of his teachers, who was upset with Junior for not applying himself in class. I attempted to explain the situation, and it fell on deaf ears. I didn't have the social skills to make the situation clear.

I had always wanted to be a football coach. After my friend's death occurred, I was driven to become a teacher instead. It occurred to me that life is more than winning and losing football games. Our real gift is to assist students to become responsible, successful citizens. I decided to own this.

My direction is for every student to have a post-high school plan of action, based upon their interests.

Think through your own story, and tap into your purpose. You will then negotiate from the strength of this commitment.

CHAPTER 8

THE ELEPHANT IN THE ROOM

The elephant: a huge issue everyone sees but no one acknowledges.

We know that the clearer the direction of the organization, and the clearer the roles individuals play in achieving that direction, overall performance of the organization will improve. If a superintendent has the belief they need to check with the board before making the smallest of decisions, we have an "elephant" in the room. As a superintendent we need to seek out whether our employees know *their* role in achieving district direction, and if they know the authority they have in doing their job. With every employee who clearly knows the direction of their job and the authority they have to make decisions, the more effective the district will be.

NOT A FIT

I remember being an assistant principal with a new assistant superintendent of educational services. It was the most frustrating time of my career. I had several thoughts for programs and practices I wanted to implement. The principal I worked with was about to retire, and he recommended I seek approval of the new assistant superintendent, as he felt he would be the next superintendent when our current superintendent decided to retire (and this did occur.)

I did seek his permission to develop five programs, and he said, "No" to all of them. Unfortunately, I did not understand the direction for my position or the authority I had to make decisions. It was a guessing game, and I became increasingly frustrated.

Listening was not his strength. He preferred *top down* bureaucratic leadership. I had the distinct feeling that he couldn't understand why I didn't know what he was thinking, and why I had all these ideas he didn't like. A personal friend of mine, who was an elementary principal in the district, told me that she would stop by his office and ask what he was working on. Whereupon he would pontificate his ideas to her, and then she would say, "Now that is a great idea." At the next elementary principals meeting she would suggest the very idea he told her about, and he would say, "Now that is a great idea."

He wanted what he wanted, but unfortunately for me, I never understood what he wanted, and *that was on me*. I was too busy thinking of my ideas and not listening to him to understand his direction. It was during this time I decided it would be in my best interest to leave the district, and I was fortunate enough to secure a principal position in another district.

Later when I became a superintendent I made sure our principals knew their direction and the authority each school had to make educational decisions to improve student learning.

No one changes until it hurts. His style and my style were not a fit. I'm not faulting him. I just knew I needed a different style of leadership to excel.

LESSON LEARNED

This is what I love about America. No one can force you to stay in a job. I moved on, as was my right, and the assistant superintendent did not have to change for me, as was his right, and he did become the next superintendent. I took a risk by leaving the district and for me, it paid off.

I had come to a fork in the road, and I took the road less traveled by and that made all the difference.

~Robert Frost, 1916

TYPICAL RESPONSE

I never addressed the elephant in the room; I simply left. This is a typical response as employees tend to leave their immediate supervisor and not the company (Buckingham & Coffman, 1999). Superintendents will leave boards; teachers will leave principals.

FORK IN THE ROAD

Now take this back to the superintendent level. If you want to go in a direction the board doesn't want you to, you have come to a fork in the road. Your options are:

- ♦ Wait for the next board election to possibly get new board members

- ♦ Seek other employment

- ♦ Confront the board, risking possible loss of employment

- ♦ Discuss with the board and possibly reach a middle ground

- ♦ Have a third party facilitator do a series of organizational effectiveness workshops

- ♦ Submit to the board's direction and implement their suggestions

As a new superintendent, if the board wants you to do a task that you disagree with, adopt a positive attitude and get it done. This will build trust with the board and hopefully allow you to do your pet projects down the road.

The only things to dig your heels in and refuse to do are those that are:

♦ Illegal

♦ Immoral

♦ Unethical

An example that touches on all three happened when a superintendent informed me that he and his board president were in Washington D.C., lobbying for federal dollars. The board president wanted to know—could he charge something illegal on the district credit card? Answer? That would be No, No, and *NO!*

So what is the elephant in the room? Role Confusion. You have the title, but you don't have the authority. Most superintendents do not have an employment contract that clearly and unambiguously defines the authority, duties and latitude they have to lead a school district.

> *"Complex organizations require strong, knowledgeable executive leadership to get everyone pulling in the same direction" (Bader & Associates, 2008).*

The job is difficult enough even with great contract language so we need to limit the potential problems from the start.

A new superintendent will know something isn't right but they can't put their finger on it. It is the elephant in the room blocking their vision. The superintendent would be wise just to say, "It will be impossible to effectively lead this district, as I don't know my authority." The superintendent candidate needs to call the board's attention to the fact that the contract language is a huge ELEPHANT that will promote failure.

What does the contract say? You need to state the obvious; the language is often ambiguous at best, or gives all authority to make decisions to the board, thus rendering the superintendent ineffectual. You would be served best if you have contract language that causes a board to pause and consider your authority as "....current board members are more self-centered...want quick fixes and are very demanding of the superintendent's time" (Mountford, 2004).

Even when boards have the best intentions this is harmful, most importantly to student learning, and also to the relationship between the board and superintendent. Before you sign the contract, take the time to clarify your duties, responsibilities and authority. Most superintendents don't take the time because the board doesn't want to take the time to discuss it; they needed you on the job yesterday.

THE MOST CRITICAL ELEMENT IN THE CONTRACT

Ann McColl, who in 2000 was general counsel to the North Carolina Association of Administrators stated, *"The provisions that establish the working relationship between the board and superintendent may be the most critical element in a superintendent's contract."*

Assistant Professor Meredith Mountford in 2004 said, *"Perhaps the single issue that causes superintendent dismissal is role confusion as to the board-superintendent working relationship."*

Governance consultants Randy Quinn and Linda Dawson of the Aspen Group suggested in 2011,*"A major reason for superintendent turnover is the dysfunctional relationships that develop because of communication problems caused by role confusion."*

There it is! The elephant in the room is "role confusion." We have an attorney, a college professor, and a governance consulting group all pointing to role confusion in the working relationship between the board and superintendent that can lead to superintendent dismissal.

What is the board's perspective? *"The fewer the written obligations the better"* (Board attorney Steve Zweig).

Role confusion is certainly better for board power and authority, but certainly not for superintendent and board *effectiveness*. As the district stalls into mediocrity the board will hold the superintendent accountable, leading to dismissal. *The average board simply does not understand effective leadership practices; yet they do fear losing power and control.*

NOW YOU KNOW

The elephant can no longer hide in plain sight! Boards are advised by legal counsel that if they are going to put something in writing to draft it as a *policy*, because they can change policy at any time. Their reasoning is that if it is put into a superintendent's contract, it will handcuff a future board's ability to control the superintendent.

In California there is an education code provision E.C. 35020 that states "the governing board shall fix duties to be performed by all persons in public school service in the district." I would suggest to superintendents to use their state Education Code to discuss with the board their responsibility as a board to clearly define your duties and authority to perform those duties.

Now that you know the importance of superintendent authority it is time to address the elephant in the room and refuse any contract offer that does not clearly state your duties and authority to make decisions. It is for the good of the district and for students' education.

You want basic contract language that reflects something as follows:

Superintendent Duties: Shall have the authority to manage the day to day decisions of the district to achieve Board direction, goals and objectives to include:

* To organize or reorganize the administrative or management staff

* To assign principals to their schools and to be able to transfer or demote management personnel

* To administer all programs; funds; personnel; facilities; contracts

* To attend all board meetings, including closed sessions, except closed sessions to discuss termination of the superintendent.

When you negotiate a comprehensive contract at the beginning of your relationship with the board, it can serve as training for the board as to their role if you make it a "living contract". This simply means that at least once each year you schedule a third party facilitated workshop, preferably on a Saturday, to review the document for understanding—not to renegotiate the contract.

A DYSFUNCTIONAL BOARD AND BOARD OVERREACH

A board becomes dysfunctional when it, individually or collectively, engages in directing or questioning the day to day decisions and operational detail of running a district that interferes or countermands a superintendent's decisions. Collaboration between the board and superintendent is essential to the success of a district. Knowing who has final authority to make a decision is a necessity to improving the speed and quality of the decision.

BOARDS AT THEIR BEST

A board functions best when it sets very clear strategic direction: expectations, goals and objectives for the superintendent. The superintendent will then devise a plan to marshal resources, assign personnel, make decisions, and communicate the plan to the board to accomplish the board's direction.

THE BOARD'S ROLE FOCUSES ON:

♦ Setting long term strategic direction for the district

♦ Monitoring progress on objectives

♦ Monitoring how management is keeping the board informed, so that the board never feels removed from what the management team is doing and how they are making their decisions.

♦ Monitoring how management is implementing board policy

♦ Monitoring administrative budget efficiency and improving student learning

♦ Monitoring compliance with state and federal regulations

♦ Monitoring how management collects and uses community and staff input

♦ Evaluating superintendent performance

"Monitoring organizational performance should be a significant component of the board's job...." (Dawson & Quinn, 2000). *A highly effective board is fixated on the "ends" or results they want you to obtain and leave the details up to you.* The board is not the superintendent and the superintendent is not the board. In a highly effective board-superintendent team, the board would set a clear focused future direction of the district after receiving input from a collaborative system developed in consultation with the superintendent. The superintendent would then establish a plan, assign personnel, and marshal the resources necessary to achieve the boards direction while in consultation with the board.

Both the superintendent and board have clear roles. The high performing board-superintendent team keeps each other informed and respects each other's input. They work as a team, with the superintendent recognizing that the board is ultimately responsible for the direction of the district and the board recognizing that the superintendent is ultimately responsible to set the operational plan to achieve the board's direction.

COUNTING THE VOTES

One caveat: in most contracts it takes *just* a majority vote of the board to remove the superintendent. Therefore, sometimes discretion is the better part of valor. If the majority or total board is against your decision I recommend you just *listen for understanding* as opposed to defending, arguing, and/or lobbying for your point of view. It won't matter if you are out of a job.

CHAPTER 9

EFFECTIVE BOARDS AND GREAT BOARD MEMBERS

Do what is right, not what is politically expedient.

I have known and worked for outstanding people who have made a major contribution to their community by serving on a school board. They are first and foremost humanitarians, wanting the best for children and staff. They possess strength of character and are exceptionally resilient at bouncing back from problems. They serve as a role models and make us better people by working for them. They are skilled, as Rudyard Kipling wrote in his poem "If," at "*treating triumph and disaster the same.*" They are not impressed or upset by either circumstance and do not get emotionally hijacked. Under their calm exterior they have a steely sense of resolve to do what is right for the situation not for what is politically expedient. Together with other dedicated people they create effective boards of education.

> *Effective boards create conditions for superintendents to do their best work (Daniel Pink, Drive, 2009).*

Effective boards are extremely focused on results, and how they lead and achieve results is radically different than boards who fail to achieve.

EFFECTIVE BOARDS ARE REMARKABLE COACHES

They understand they want you at your best to deliver what they want for their district. This is why they are interested in what makes you perform your best. You are their star player, and they are the coaches of the team. With this mindset they want you to produce results. Whatever results these may be, they want you to produce. To produce, you need to be at your best without pointless distractions. Effective boards do not put up roadblocks to your leadership. They are always monitoring and coaching to see what you need to be at the top of your leadership game.

A new principal I hired was doing poorly. In a discussion with the board president I stated that I blew it when I hired him. She countered, "You made the best selection from the available candidates." This caused me to reflect and it lifted my spirits. Great board members are remarkable coaches.

LEADERSHIP MATTERS

Effective boards are great leaders. They understand that they have one employee- the superintendent and that it is their responsibility to create a work environment whereby the superintendent can be most successful.

They lead by understanding they desire power *with* the superintendent not power *over* the superintendent (Terez, 2007).

Pay close attention to contract language regarding EVALUATION: The Board shall annually evaluate the superintendent's performance using mutually agreed upon objectives. Language that represents a Board that desires POWER OVER the superintendent will state language such as: The Board shall determine the goals and objectives and the evaluation format for the superintendent.

CONTRACT NEGOTIATIONS

Effective boards negotiate to create a work environment for you to do your best work. They want you to be provided what you need to successfully lead their district with as few disruptions as possible. They will ask:

"What do you need in your contract that will allow you to do your best work for our district?" They don't view you as a teacher, and they expect your contract to be materially different from the teacher's negotiated agreement. You are not a teacher. You are the CEO, and they understand the difference.

Consider this point. What does it take for you to perform at your best? Effective boards want to know this, and you should reflect upon this to be able to explain it to them during the contract negotiation process. Effective boards will have no problem accepting your contract although they may have difficulty financing your requests. We have to be prudent when a board states, "We cannot afford your requests." Dysfunctional boards state their contract is a take it or leave it offer.

The problem for a rookie superintendent candidate is that they don't know what they haven't experienced. Seasoned superintendents have an endless memory of all the things that occur to disrupt their leadership ability. It is at this moment the phrase "trust me" comes to mind.

EFFECTIVE BOARD BEHAVIORS

Boards that outperform others eliminate barriers to leadership, provide feedback, inspire confidence, share information and welcome new ideas (Bassi & McMurrer, 2007). They speak with one voice and support the decisions of the full board without participating in "hallway chatter". They are united. They don't always agree and can strongly voice objections in closed session, but through it all they are a *team*. They know their role in the district is to focus on future direction and not meddle in the day to day issues of running a district.

EFFECTIVE BOARDS know what they want in a leader. When you are first hired they will inform you, "This is why we hired you" and will state the behaviors, characteristics, and results you have achieved and that they desire for their district. They know exactly what they want in a leader, and they thoroughly vetted you to know how you will lead their district.

Effective Boards will have Board Protocols (see Chapter 11) or standards of conduct and hold themselves accountable. They will regularly discuss their protocols at board meetings. They have high standards for themselves as well as high standards for the superintendent.

EFFECTIVE BOARDS have a clear direction. They have a clear vision and expect the superintendent to draft a plan and marshal the resources to achieve it. They diligently monitor the superintendent's plan to achieve their vision. They vigorously question and put to proof the superintendent's actions, causing the superintendent to grow professionally as a direct result of their proactive leadership.

EFFECTIVE BOARDS collaborate with the superintendent. Even though they know they have the authority to create the direction for the district they have a keen interest in the superintendent's point of view.

See Chapter 12, contract item #21: "Every 4 months the superintendent shall report to the board, in closed session, progress on meeting evaluation objectives." An effective board wants an ongoing dialogue with the superintendent

EFFECTIVE BOARDS confront problems and problem people. Effective boards have tremendous empathy for others, and yet they confront problems and problem people the same way—directly and professionally. They understand their first priority is to students. They do not let friendship with staff members get in the way of allowing the superintendent to do the job or interfere with their ability to make a decision.

See Chapter 13, contract item #14, Superintendent Duties: The board clearly states the authority of the superintendent. For example: The superintendent has the authority to manage the day to day decisions of the district, assign principals to their schools, etc.

An ineffective board will have a disclaimer to mitigate your authority. This is language you need to avoid: "Superintendent has the authority to manage the day to day decisions of the district <u>with the approval of the board</u>. This phrase erases all superintendent authority.

You need to know what authority you actually have, as employees need one supervisor. If you need to clear most or all decisions through the board, employees will stop listening to you and go directly to the board.

THE POWER OF THE MESSAGE

As a leader, the power of the message is important. Effective boards understand the complexity and demands on the superintendent and focus on keeping their employee motivated. They communicate their belief in the superintendent. They have the uncanny knack of keeping the superintendent's head in the game and don't let them get sidetracked by politics.

EFFECTIVE BOARDS are master motivators. My favorite illustrative story on motivation is about Reggie Jackson, the former major league baseball player. When he played for the Yankees, the owner got down on Reggie and took it out on him in the newspapers, constantly criticizing his performance. At the end of the season, Reggie didn't post great numbers and he was traded to the Oakland A's. At the end of his first season with the A's, he was honored to be selected as the league MVP.

From outhouse to penthouse: I remember a sports reporter asking Reggie Jackson what caused the turnaround in his performance. Reggie said, "The Oakland A's coach asked me what I wanted, and I told him, 'I want to make a contribution to the team.' *The coach believed in me."*

Wow! Professional baseball players have great speed, reflexes, and coordination, and yet a negative owner of the New York Yankees could drastically reduce player's skill set through negative messages. Conversely, the next coach communicated his belief in Reggie, and he became the best in baseball.

In the same way, effective boards motivate by communicating their belief in the superintendent's leadership.

BIG PICTURE

EFFECTIVE BOARDS are made from great people. They understand that positive reinforcement produces greater results than negativity. They are focused on the big picture and don't get lost in the weeds of the superintendent's job tasks. Through their leadership they model how they want the superintendent to lead.

For example, you can present the following illustration to effective boards, and they understand it instantly: "Imagine you (the school board) are the president of the United States at the end of WWII. You direct General Eisenhower (the superintendent) by saying, "The American people desire world peace and to end this war." General Eisenhower (the superintendent) responds, "To achieve world peace, I need to bomb Hiroshima."

EFFECTIVE BOARDS understand that to accomplish great things it is necessary to make difficult decisions. In education we will never be faced with such a soul-shaking decision. Yet this illustration of the problem is meant to create a contrast with the mindset of ineffective board members, who wouldn't get it. While Ike was addressing problems and directing his staff to create world peace, the clueless board member would interrupt the meeting to point out that the sprinklers out front aren't working.

MAKES YOU WANT TO HOLLER

EFFECTIVE BOARDS don't get lost in the weeds of the job, and they model that they don't want the superintendent to get involved in the weeds of staff member's jobs. What is most impressive about the effective boards is how they behave. They don't publically criticize or put down the superintendent. They question and provide counsel. They publically praise and privately criticize.

One board member remembered when he received a staff report prepared for a board meeting. The report contained spelling and grammatical errors. To him, it was an example of unprofessional work, and at the board meeting he called attention to it during public session. This action humiliated staff and also served as a bullying tactic. Upon reflection, he thought the better course of action would have been to voice his concern to the superintendent when he received the report before the meeting (Mayer, 2011).

ADVISE, DON'T CRITICIZE

EFFECTIVE BOARDS are diligent and don't blindly trust the superintendent. They will ask for the plan to achieve their vision and ask questions such as, "Have you thought about…?""How long do you figure it will take…?" "What are some things that could hinder your action plan…?"

EFFECTIVE BOARDS look in the mirror. When things go wrong their first response is not to *blame*, but to ask themselves, "What could we have done differently as a board, to produce better results from our superintendent?" *This is the board we would work for without a contract.* They make us better people and model for us how they want the district to be led. These are the great public servants in America. We may not always agree with their politics, but we will always admire and respect their humanity and most importantly, their leadership.

I suggest you make certain there is a description of board policy direction in your contract. (See Chapter 13, contract item #16, Board Policy Direction Defined.) Without this language, there are some board members who believe the superintendent must do anything they, as a board, direct. You want to spell out your authority, or you could very easily have a board taking action at a board meeting that directs you who to hire or transfer or discipline. Remember, the more comprehensive your contract language, the more effective the board and superintendent team.

CHAPTER 10

ROGUE BOARD MEMBERS

The key to winning is poise under stress.
~Mark Goulston, 2009

I have worked with great school boards and even greater individual board members. I always knew we were united on our purpose, and I trusted in and respected their advice and counsel. I would have gladly worked for them without a contract. It was genuinely a team effort, born of the mutual respect and trust that is so necessary to propel a district to being effective for *all* students.

This book is not written with great boards in mind, as no book would be necessary. It is written with the knowledge that some individual board members are "rogue" board members.

Mark Goulston, in his book *Just Listen*, gave the following description of people to avoid. Unfortunately when they are board members we need to up our game—starting with the employment contract—as it is impossible to avoid them.

♦ Toxic; they just want to destroy authority figures

♦ Bullies; they come after you, as they see you as easy prey

♦ Narcissists, whose catch phrase is, "Enough about you,

let's talk about me." They will never give you credit for your leadership.

♦ Needy; it is one crisis after another and you will always fail them.

♦ Psychopathic; they are cold blooded. One in a hundred people are psychopathic. The rule is to get away even if it means chewing off your leg to escape.

In addition to these I would like to add my own to the list:

♦ Political Opportunists; whose catch phrase is "This is nothing personal…" as they make a statement that has nothing to do with education, but is designed to advance their sights on the city council, on their way to the state assembly.

Rogue board members have two things in common. First, they are not a member of the board-superintendent team. They serve as a stand-alone separate board, only going along with the full board vote when it meets their needs. Second, they will throw you under the bus in the next beat of your heart, just after giving you a compliment.

The best part in becoming a superintendent is getting to know yourself, as you will be put in situations that will help you discover values you didn't know you had. As superintendent you will have the best moment in your career and the worst moment in your career, and they can both occur in the same minute.

NEVER BE A VICTIM

What does this mean, to "never be a victim?" It is the martyr syndrome to say *"I sacrifice myself for you."* When confronted with rogue board members, some superintendents will hang on and play the victim, encouraged by sympathetic staff members who extoll how much they appreciate what you do for them. Next thing you know the board is buying you out. This is the point where you realize the importance of a strong financial package to protect yourself and your family.

PROTECT YOURSELF AT ALL TIMES

Take this moment to reflect on your basic wants and needs to be a superintendent. Do you want to accomplish something for students, or do you need recognition and to be popular?

What is my point? Don't be a hero and don't behave as a victim. Recognize when you have come to a fork in the road and be prepared to move on. That is being a leader. I have observed superintendents retiring and wanting to be loved by staff and students. Five years later the new staff members will exclaim, "What was your name again?" The veteran staff members will virtually ignore you as they "cotton on" to the new superintendent. Why? This is politics. "What have you done for me lately?" You don't want to get yourself in the position where you need the staff more than they need you.

LESSON TO LEARN

You want to lead a successful district, improving student education and improving the quality of life for staff. Then move on or retire. For those who are fortunate enough to retire — also learn to let go and to allow the next superintendent to lead — their way.

Keep your friends close and your enemies closer. Never—<u>never</u> show negative emotion or speak negatively about this person, as he has people who respect him.

A new, small district superintendent complained that the former retired superintendent wouldn't let go of the position. He lived in the community, attended student events, interacted with staff and detailed how he would handle situations, etc. He was not allowing the new superintendent to become a trusted leader because of his interference. I suggested two courses of action: (1) Look for a new job or, (2) work with the former superintendent by meeting regularly with him for his counsel.

IT'S ALL ABOUT THE BOARD

Always keep your resume up to date and aggressively look for a new job when you have two rogue board members. This usually occurs in your second or third board as they didn't hire you and tend to want new leadership.

For the effective board, it is all about preserving the board. They speak with one voice. For rogue board members, it is all about *them*. They serve as a stand-alone board, unwilling to compromise and proud to vote "no" on any item they don't agree to. *One bad apple spoils the barrel.* Without a comprehensive contract, these bad apple board members will get you to "talk to yourself, then to argue with yourself, and finally to lose those arguments." They will have you going in so many circles that you will become emotionally and mentally exhausted. They make up the rogue board members as they create angst, not only for you, but for other board members as well. It takes a veteran and sophisticated board to counter the effects of a rogue board member.

BOUNDED RATIONALITY

I have heard more than one superintendent talking to themselves, usually doubting themselves when they thought no one was within ear shot. I don't know the explanation for this behavior- perhaps it is born from a feeling of not being in control and trying to sort things out.

Your security is your employment contract. The superintendent employment contract defines the rules of your role as the leader of the district. In sports we must define the field of play; without this detail there would be chaos. Imagine a football game without an end zone, or a track meet without a finish line. This is called "bounded rationality." Simply stated, we put boundaries around a concept so that everyone understands how things work.

This is the purpose of your contract. It serves to make clear the "boundaries" between you and the board. The goal is to have both the board and superintendent fully understand how things work between the parties. In this way we prevent either party from blurring the boundaries and causing role confusion.

See Chapter 12, Sample Contract item #15, Board Responsibilities. I suggest language that states, "The Board shall not take an action that violates the authority of the superintendent as stated within this contract." Again, this is the reason you want your authority defined, as without it there will be a Board member wo tries to direct you to do what they want. If you spell out your authority in the contract, the other Board members will simply refer to your contract and say, "That is not our job."

CHAPTER 11

TEAM PROTOCOLS

"When education is placed in the hands of a master leader amazing things can happen" Quinn, 1996.

Most boards will have a *code of conduct policy* or *protocols* that define professional behavior expectations of one another. You can do a quick review of their policy manual (usually online) to see if these are in place before an interview. If they have them, the next question is, do they use them?

This is an example of "bounded rationality," as you are attempting to define the playing field so that everyone can work together as a high functioning team.

If they do not have a code of conduct or protocols it would be wise to add language to your contract that the board either agrees to the following protocols, or agrees to work with the superintendent to create their own. The next step is to make them "come to life" instead of allowing them to recede like wallpaper, where no one pays any attention to them.

Why is it important for the board and superintendent to work as a team? Teams achieve greater results than people working as individuals (Johnson & Johnson, 2000).

SAMPLE PROTOCOLS

BYLAWS OF THE BOARD BB 9005(A)

BOARD- SUPERINTENDENT PROTOCOLS

The purpose of board-superintendent protocols is to provide an essential set of professional guidelines by which the members of the board- superintendent team are to function so that employees receive a clear message to follow.

The board-superintendent team acknowledges that they are the district's most visible representatives and they are required to maintain higher standards of personal conduct than all other employees. In order to represent the district with integrity and high ethical standards, the board-superintendent team shall avoid professional or personal situations that might reflect negatively on the district (CSBA, 2016).

I inserted the paragraph above from a 2016 CSBA sample superintendent contract as I thought it had implications not only for the superintendent, but for the board as well. When these statements are reviewed by board members, it may have a sobering impact on some of the rogue behaviors or give the other Board members the strength to deal with ineffective behaviors.

COMMUNICATION

1. During a meeting, board members, when interacting with the public, will not make statements that could be interpreted as having full-team concurrence.

2. Never will a matter be brought to a public meeting that is a surprise to a board member.

3. All board members are to be apprised in a timely manner of any incident that they may be called upon to answer or explain.

4. Questions and clarification of board agenda items are to be communicated to the superintendent prior to the board meeting, if at all possible.

5. Irritations will be communicated as soon as possible to prevent aggravating the situation.

6. Any concern reported to the superintendent by a board member is to receive the highest priority, with the disposition of the matter communicated to all of the team.

7. All significant administrative actions are to be communicated to all board members.

8. All team members have a unique responsibility to share pertinent information that they see and hear regarding the district.

9. Information communicated to one board member shall be given to all board members.

10. The team has the responsibility to educate the district and community regarding the roles of team members.

11. The superintendent will provide alternatives, options, and rationales for decisions requiring board action.

TEAMWORK

1. Each member of the team is dedicated to making all other members of the team successful.

2. No individual board member will make or appear to make a decision that appropriately should be made by the entire board.

3. Board meeting attendance and punctuality are to be given the highest priority.

4. No one is to poll the board members or use influence to create discord among them.

5. No individual team member will ever use the media as a forum.

6. Loyalty to the entire team includes:

    ○ Giving one's opinion on all issues. Silence equals agreement

    ○ Refraining from bad-mouthing other team members, particularly in public

    ○ Respecting each individual's opinion

    ○ Accepting and supporting the action of the team

7. Unintentional mistakes may occur and should not be attributed to unwillingness to be a team player.

8. Every action by a member of the team should be directed toward improving the educational program for students. If not, it is not to be taken.

9. The team acknowledges the importance of flexibility in adjusting priorities and areas of focus to meet changing needs.

10. Openly considering options and alternatives is recognized as a vehicle of good decision-making.

11. All team members are to work toward being open-minded to changes that break traditions but may move the district forward.

12. It is the responsibility of each board member to help the superintendent and every other team member be successful.

13. It is the responsibility of each board member to interface with other board members on a social level, to gain better insight into the thinking of their colleagues.

14. Board member conversations with staff are to be constructive and edifying, not gossiping, complaining, or criticizing.

CHAIN OF COMMAND

1. All will define and understand the difference between administration and policymaking and respect the roles of each other.

2. Individual member requests for reports, surveys, projects, etc., will be directed only to the superintendent, who, depending upon staff load, may ask for a board vote prior to committing district resources.

3. Promotional appointments of administrators are made by the superintendent, but only in consultation with the board.

4. Personnel changes are to be recommended by the superintendent. Board input will include only significant and relevant data—never the "pushing" or "pushing out" of individuals.

5. As a general premise, unsubstantiated rumor, innuendo, and information from anonymous sources are not to receive

attention by anyone but the superintendent, who will investigate and report. The board has the discretion to determine the most appropriate means to conduct an investigation.

6. Any complaint made to a board member by the community is to be referred directly to the superintendent, who is to resolve it according to board policy.

7. No individual board member is to come between the superintendent and his/her staff.

8. All substantive contacts, including phone calls, between a board member and staff or community are to be reported to the superintendent as soon as possible.

9. The district's complaint procedures are to be used and reinforced, to allow those closest to a concern the opportunity to solve it.

10. Every appointment and promotion is to be done according to policy, with the board acting on the recommendation from the superintendent. There is to be no interference by the board.

11. The board president is the spokesperson for the board when issuing public statements. To the extent possible, the board president will seek consensus of the board. The board president may give direction, if appropriate, to the superintendent to issue statements on the board's behalf.

RESPECT AND DECORUM

1. All conversation taking place in closed sessions will remain absolutely confidential with the exception of reporting requirements according to the Brown Act.

2. Each member of the team is to be treated with dignity and respect.

3. Every member of the team is honorable, honest, and dedicated to the success of the team.

4. Operate openly, with trust and integrity.

5. Board members, as their time permits, are encouraged to visit school sites and attend school functions, but will avoid interrupting instruction unnecessarily or interrupting employees at work.

6. Grandstanding or "playing to the audience" is inappropriate behavior.

7. Individual personnel issues are not to be discussed in open session.

8. Never will some board members conspire against other board members.

9. The points of view of each member deserve to be heard, as long as they do not violate the protocols or core values of the district.

Source: Adapted from the work of Dr. Norm Eisen, (2004) deceased former superintendent. He compiled a list of protocols after consulting with several boards. Dr. Ralph Baker added the headings for each section in 2010.

An effective annual strategy is to have the Board select twelve protocols; one per month, to work on throughout the year. Have one protocol listed on each board agenda and assign a board member to lead a discussion on it with the other board members.

All protocols are still in effect. The Board is selecting the protocols they would like to focus on throughout the year. The board will be modeling the professional behavior they desire of district employees.

CHAPTER 12

SAMPLE CONTRACT WITH NEGOTIATING NOTES

Treat your contract as a living document that is integral to successfully leading a district. You will want to refer to it as much or more than you refer to the District Policy Manuals.

Make certain you check with your state administrative association and your school district legal counsel as to the legality of your contract.

Provide a copy of your contract to your personnel department and your business department, as well as keeping a personal copy at home for your records.

SUPERINTENDENT EMPLOYMENT CONTRACT

BETWEEN THE BOARD OF TRUSTEES OF THE SCHOOL DISTRICT

AND SUPERINTENDENT

This contract is entered into as of this 1st day of July 20__, between the Board of Trustees (hereinafter referred to as the "Board") of and on behalf of the XYZ School District (hereinafter referred to as the "District") and Superintendent (hereinafter referred to as the "Superintendent").

Now therefore the above named parties hereby mutually agree as follows:

BOARD-SUPERINTENDENT BELIEF STATEMENT

The Board has one employee—the superintendent, and the Board believes a high-performing Board-superintendent team has the greatest impact on student education because of the authority vested in these positions. Teamwork is not sharing decisions between the Board and the superintendent it is sharing complimentary yet separate roles. The Board knows the position of superintendent has the highest turnover rate in education, making it the most vulnerable position within the district. For these reasons, the Board believes it is necessary to clearly define the duties of the superintendent and the Board to serve as a basis for effective communication and teamwork in the management of the school district. By doing so the Board believes this will enhance superintendent stability, longevity, and effectiveness, improving the overall quality of the educational program and the operational success of the district.

Note: This is an optional, bold statement, to emphasize that it is a board-superintendent team that is responsible for student learning. Effective boards will have no problem with this statement. Less effective boards will have a problem with it. I suggest you use this as a discussion tool between you and the board to clarify that the board and superintendent have separate roles, and to discuss what that means.

1. **Superintendent, Chief Executive Officer of the Governing Board, Secretary for the Board:** Superintendent is employed as the superintendent of the School District. (S)He shall also be the Chief Executive Officer of the Governing Board and shall serve as the secretary for the Board.

Note 1. Having the CEO reference is important, as I know of a board member in a district who refuted this claim. He said the board was the CEO. That is role confusion, from the start. Negotiating this distinction clarified the issue.

2. **Term:** ____ years. Beginning July 1, 20__, the Board employs the Superintendent for a period of ____ years terminating on June 30, 20__.

Note 2. You want the maximum years allowed by state law, to send a message of confidence to staff and community that the board is all in with you leading the district. Contracts for less than the maximum send a message that the Board is not sure you are the right choice.

If a board is adamant about not giving a maximum term contract first ask them <u>why</u> and then ask "What would you need to provide me a maximum term contract?" If they specify it, put that language into the contract. A usual reason is the board feels you need to prove yourself first; they don't want to be viewed by the voters as being an easy boss who gave away the store to an unproven superintendent.

3. **Reassignment:** The Superintendent is employed specifically and solely to perform the duties as Superintendent of schools for the district. The Superintendent cannot be reassigned from the position as Superintendent to another position without the Superintendent's written authorization.

Note 3. For your protection from a vindictive board that would reassign you to another position rather than buying you out. This is a board that wants you to earn every last penny.

4.   **Amendment of Agreement:** This agreement shall only be changed, modified or amended by mutual consent of the parties.

Note 4. Protects you from the Board that believes they have the authority to do whatever they want with a majority vote of the Board and you do not have a say in the process. Don't let them own you.

5.   **Contract Renewal:** On or before March 15, 20__ the Superintendent shall submit to the Board a new contract proposal. The Board will have until June 15, 20__, to respond to the proposal. If the Board does not respond to the proposal, the current terms and conditions remain in effect until the contract's termination date.

Note 5. Provide language in the contract that extends your contract for an additional year if you receive a satisfactory evaluation. The language should be clear, and the contract extension must be approved by the board in the form of an amendment at a regularly scheduled meeting (Almond et al., 2016).

The usual contract starts July 1. It is best if you start negotiating prior to 12 months remaining on your contract. If the Board does not respond to negotiating a new contract you will know you have 12 months to find a new job until your contract ends. Some Boards want to work you as long as they can and then release you. Protect yourself at all times.

Unacceptable language would be if the Board wants to go by the legal minimum notice of 45 days prior to the end of your contract. (A 45 day notice may vary between states.) It is nearly impossible to find another position in 45 days. Read this language carefully and protect your ability to secure another position, as you do not want to be forced out with too short a notice and too small a buyout to secure other employment.

6. **Intellectual Property:** Any and all inventions, discoveries, developments, innovations, programs or practices conceived by the Superintendent relative to the duties under this agreement shall be the exclusive property of the superintendent.

Note 6. Some boards will state that they shall retain exclusive rights to anything you develop. Think of a possible program you might create; you will want to retain the rights to that program.

7. **Consulting/ Conflict of interest:** The Superintendent shall be permitted to undertake consulting, writing, teaching, and speaking engagements so long as these do not interfere with the performance of the duties as Superintendent. Any consulting work undertaken by the Superintendent for compensation must be taken on vacation days, personal days, holidays or non-duty days. The Superintendent shall comply with regulations regarding a conflict of interest. The aforementioned prohibition shall include, without limitation holding a pecuniary (financial) interest in any property, product or service provided to or being considered to be provided to the District.

Note 7. The Board determines if any work you are doing interferes with you doing the job of superintendent. Make sure you communicate to the Board any and all work you do outside of the District. Make certain you are not paid by the District when you are also being paid by another party to do work for them. Communication is key.

8. **Termination Without Cause:** The Board may terminate this Agreement with a super-majority vote of the Board at a regularly scheduled Board meeting. If the Board seeks to terminate this contract, the cash and benefit settlement shall be the amount of time left on the contract or

the maximum allowed by law whichever is less. The buyout provision remains in force if the Superintendent secures other employment within the amount of time left on the contract.

Note 8. You want language that states if you find employment within the 12 month buyout period the board shall continue to pay until the 12 month buyout period ends. Why? Because they have injured you.

a.   If the Board exercises *termination without cause* they agree they shall not speak negatively about the Superintendent in any public or private meeting. This is defined as a meeting between one or more people or on social media.

Note 8a. Ideally you and the board will draft a letter of recommendation citing your accomplishments. They agree to cite it if asked by a prospective employer, and you can use it in your job search. One suggestion would be for you to draft a copy of what you would like the board to write and present it to the board president.

9.   **Termination for Just Cause:** The Superintendent shall only be terminated for just cause. Should the Board elect to pursue termination for just cause; the Board must first provide Superintendent with a statement detailing the incidents of malfeasance and give Superintendent six months to demonstrate improvement. If the Board elects the option to terminate this Agreement with just cause, it must do so by taking action at a *regularly scheduled board* meeting with a *supermajority vote* of the Board.

Note 9. Getting language such as Just Cause for Malfeasance and super-majority vote of the Board is rare. But you don't get what you don't ask for. A fallback position is to ask for this during the first 2 years, as you will make mistakes as a new superintendent and would like some protection during this critical time. "I would appreciate the Board allowing this language in the first two years of the contract as I need some employment security."

Stronger language would be to have *binding arbitration* language for Termination for Cause. Example: "Any controversy arising out of or relating to this Contract, its enforcement or interpretation, or because of an alleged breach, default, or misrepresentation in connection with any of its provisions, or any other controversy arising out of the Superintendent's employment, including, but not limited to, any state or federal statutory claims, shall be submitted to binding arbitration in Los Angeles County, California, before a sole arbitrator selected from Judicial Arbitration and Mediation Services, Inc., Los Angeles County, California, or its successor."

If there is a strong pushback from the board, you may want to counter for this language to be in effect during the first two years of the contract, and then it will revert to super-majority vote for termination. *Be creative!*

10. **Abuse of Power/Termination For Cause:** Abuse of power: If the Superintendent is placed on paid leave, or if her/his legal defense in a criminal trial is paid by the District and (s)he is subsequently convicted of abusing her/his office or her/his title, (s)he must reimburse the District for her/his criminal defense.

11. **New Position:** The Superintendent must notify the Board President whenever *offered a contract* for a new position.

Note 11. Some boards want you to inform them whenever you *apply* for a position, and it is grounds for termination if you don't inform them. Some boards will inform you that if you ever apply for a job and don't get it, they will terminate you—and they have done so. Contract language is *important*.

AN OUT-OF-THE-BOX THOUGHT

You might consider language requiring you to apply for a new super-intendent position once every four years. Why would a board agree to this? It keeps all parties, you and the board, on their toes. Going through a superintendent search forces the superintendent candidate to recon-sider thoughts and values about leading an organization. For the board, it forces them to consider if they value the superintendent. It's just a thought, for the more entrepreneurial superintendent candidate.

12. **Salary/ Work Year/ Vacation Days:** The annual base salary for 20_-20_ shall be $$$$$$ with a work year of 223 days and 24 vacation days, exclusive of legal holidays.

Note 12. For each year of the term, include language that provides con-sistent salary increases. You're not asking for any more than most other staff in the district that are on a salary schedule. Having consistent sal-ary increases avoids revisiting your contract on this hot topic and it also avoids being accused of "spiking" for the purpose of enhancing your pension (Almond et al., 2016).

WORK YEAR FORMULA

Days in Year   = 365
               – 104 weekend days
               = 261 possible work days

               – 14 paid holidays (*depending on specific district*)
               = 247 possible work days

               – 24 vacation days (*depending on specific contract*)
               = 223 work days (*depending on specific contract*)

Sample superintendent contract formula from the Association of California School Administrators

The superintendent's salary and/or work year cannot be reduced *unless every employee* in the District has had their salary and/or work year reduced.

You are the superintendent responsible for the district 365 days each year. If staff takes a cut in their work year, their responsibility stops. If you take a cut in your work year, your responsibility does not stop.

Some superintendents have written into their contract that they shall substitute in the classroom x number of days per year. Again, you are the superintendent, not a teacher. Why would you ever reduce the value of the position of superintendent by taking x number of days out of your work year to be a teacher? You are stating the superintendent doesn't need to work all the current days in the contract. If substituting in the classroom is important to you, I suggest you substitute on a vacation day.

The salary shall be paid in equal monthly installments.

I prefer a 5-step, 20 year management salary schedule, similar to a teacher salary schedule, with built-in seniority and doctorate stipends.

a. The Board reserves the right to otherwise adjust the Superintendent's compensation. Any adjustment in compensation during the term of this Contract shall be only in the form of an amendment and only as mutually agreed to by and between the parties, and shall not operate as a termination of this Contract. It is further provided that, with respect to any adjustment in salary, it shall not be considered that a new Contract has been entered into or that the termination date of the existing contract has been extended.

b. The Superintendent can bank/save any and all unused vacation days and be reimbursed at her/his daily rate of pay for any unused vacation days. Her/his daily rate is determined by dividing her/his annual base salary by her/his work year (223 days). The amount of vacation days carried over shall be at the sole discretion of the Superintendent.

Note 12b. Some boards do not want you to save days to cash out at a later date at a higher rate of pay. You might substitute language that states any vacation days not used by June 30 of each year shall be reimbursed to the superintendent at the daily rate by September 1 of each year. This way the board is paying you at your current rate, not with inflated dollars perhaps 10 years down the road.

13.   **Fringe Benefits:** The Superintendent shall be accorded such fringe benefits of employment as are granted to the District's "management team" employees and:

Note 13. Fringe benefits are designed to attract and retain employees. The superintendent receives more fringe benefits as they are the most exposed to termination. It is advised to have a third party facilitator to remind the board of this fact.

a.   Technology: To maintain effective communication the district shall provide a cell phone for business and personal use and full use of all forms of technology of the Superintendent's choice (including, but not limited to computers, tablet devices, printers, fax machines, cellular and data services, etc.) plus all related charges and expenses for personal and business use.

b.   Expenses: The Superintendent shall be provided a District credit card for actual and necessary expenses incurred within the scope of employment while representing the district. Except as herein provided, the District shall provide reimbursement to the Superintendent for all actual and necessary business-related expenses as paid by the Superintendent in the conduct of her/his duties and on behalf of the District.

c. Automobile: The District shall provide the Superintendent a mutually agreeable automobile for her/his personal and professional use. The District agrees to provide a District credit card for the Superintendent to use for gas and emergency maintenance of the vehicle. The District agrees to keep the automobile maintained in good working condition and provide insurance coverage for the vehicle.

Note 13c. It is a personal choice whether to ask for a car or car allowance. In California this could fall under the STRS Creditable Compensation Regulations if a previous superintendent negotiated to roll a car allowance into salary. If that is the case, the board can no longer negotiate an auto allowance, but they can provide a car. In very small districts, the board may only offer a mileage stipend.

d. Professional Organizations/Conferences/Education: The Board shall pay for the expenses for the Superintendent as CEO to participate in professional organizations, conferences and activities at the local, county, state, and national level at the discretion of the Superintendent. The Board shall pay the Superintendent's related membership dues, fees, and expenses accordingly. The Board shall receive an annual accounting of all expenses.

Note 13d. The Board may put limits on this by having you state the organizations you want to belong to. For example: ACSA; AASA; ASCD and one local service club. The Board may also ask you to state the costs of membership. Ask your business office to do this task. Do not do this yourself, as your business staff will most likely be used to calculating these costs.

e. Sick/Personal leave (credited in advance): The Superintendent shall accrue 2 days of sick leave per month or 24 per year; 10 of which can be used as personal leave. As a continuation of benefits earned from her/his prior employer, the Superintendent shall receive a sick leave credit with the District for any and all unused accumulated leave from her/his prior employer. Said continuation benefit shall be added to the Superintendent's sick leave benefit in the first year of this agreement. The continuation benefit shall accrue upon submission of proper evidence from the prior employer of entitlement benefits.

Note 13e. Without such language you could lose all accrued sick leave from your former employer.

f. Health and Welfare Benefits: The Superintendent shall be provided the same coverage as management team employees of the District.

g. Life Insurance: The District shall pay (1%-5%) of Superintendent's salary per year for life insurance for the Superintendent. The Superintendent shall select the life insurance as well as the beneficiaries.

h. Tax Sheltered Account (TSA): The District shall pay (1%-5%) of annual salary for a TSA of the Superintendent's choice and the Superintendent shall be fully vested.

Note 13h. "Shall be fully vested" means this is your money from day one. Sometimes a board will state you do not earn this amount (become vested) until you have been employed in the district for 5 years.

A percentage is better than a fixed amount, as the increase goes up with your salary. A fixed amount must be negotiated again and again.

If the board has a problem with providing both, combine both life insurance/ TSA in a percentage of annual salary: The district shall pay (1%-5%) for a TSA and/or life insurance for the superintendent.

i. Relocation Expense: The District shall pay $20,000 for the Superintendent to relocate within the District.

j. Housing Allowance: The District shall pay $2000 per month for the life of the contract for the Superintendent to use for housing within the District.

Note 13j. There are boards that want you to reside within the district. They cannot require you to, but they can provide financial assistance. You will want to have clarification by the district's legal counsel. You want to confirm your state requirements regarding residency within the district.

k. Professional Liability/ Hold Harmless: If the Superintendent is named personally in a legal action as a result of duties undertaken on behalf of the District, the Board agrees to defend and hold harmless and indemnify the Superintendent from all demands, suits, claims, actions and legal proceedings, excluding the abuse of power clause of this contract. Legal defense shall be determined pursuant to Government Code section 995 *et seq.* In no case will individual Board members be considered personally liable for indemnifying the Superintendent against such demands, claims, suits, actions and legal proceedings.

l. Contract Retirement Audit: The District shall *fully indemnify* and provide mutually agreeable legal defense in the event of an audit of the Superintendent's employment contract or retirement income. In no case shall individual Board members be considered personally liable for indemnifying the Superintendent against such demands, claims, suits, actions and legal proceedings.

Note 13l: Fully indemnify (make whole) means that if you are audited and found to owe money, the district must pay it. Why? the board is responsible for your contract, and has legal counsel to advise them. If a mistake is made, it is on them, not you. This is also why you always want legal counsel to review your contract.

Always keep a personal record of board minutes as to approval/ minutes of your contract as well as legal counsel approval as to legality of your contract to be prepared if audited.

14. **Superintendent Duties:** The Superintendent's primary responsibility is to manage the District to implement the policy direction of the Board. The Superintendent shall be governed by and perform duties and responsibilities set forth in the laws of the State of California, formal duties as defined within this contract and by rules, regulations, policies, and advice and direction of the Board. (E.C. 35020)

The Superintendent shall *have the authority:* In discharging the Superintendent authority (s)he shall keep the Board informed with follow up and follow through communication so that the Board understands the why and how of decisions.

Note 14. The ideal is for the superintendent to have a direction to move the district, and the board has a direction they want the superintendent to take the district, and it is a match. Also it is ideal when the board wants a style of leadership that matches the superintendent's style of leadership. This would make a strong board-superintendent team. A suggestion would be to accurately clarify the direction you want to take the district to benefit students.

a. To not act on individual Board member direction, as this is a violation of the contract and grounds for termination of employment.

Note 14a. You do not want to have a Board member come to you and state, "I want this to stay between you and me." They then inform you what they want you to do. With this in your contract, you can respond, "With all due respect, that would violate my contract and subject me to termination." Language is important.

b. To manage the day to day decisions of the district to institute reforms and systemic changes as the Superintendent finds necessary in order to achieve the Boards direction, goals, and objectives.

Note 14b. It is not the board's job to get into the "how to do the job" of the superintendent They are to point the long term direction of the district. Individual board members are not to tell you that you need to take care of x-y-z. They should as a board monitor your performance and have you describe how you operationalize district functions and offer advice or counsel for you to consider. A subtle distinction, but it prevents role confusion.

c. To organize or reorganize the administrative and all management staff which in her/his judgment best serves the district.

d. To assign principals to their schools and transfer or demote existing personnel.

Note 14d. You may have noticed contract language didn't say you can promote personnel. When you promote someone that usually involves more salary, and a board must approve salary. The key is communication. The board must never be surprised to learn that you have demoted or transferred personnel, as that should have been communicated well in advance of your action.

e. To administer all programs; funds; personnel; facilities; contracts; and all other administrative and academic functions.

f. To recommend all new employees to the District or employees new to their position to the Board for their approval. The Board reserves the authority to accept or reject the Superintendent's recommendation to hire new personnel. If the Board rejects the Superintendent's final recommendation the Superintendent has the authority to make a new recommendation until it meets with Board approval.

  ◆ The Superintendent recommends employees.

  ◆ The Board has final authority to approve employees.

g. To immediately accept employee resignations for and on behalf of the Board. The resignation is final once the Superintendent signs and dates receipt of all resignations. The Superintendent shall inform the Board of all resignations at the next regular Board meeting as a personnel information item.

Note 14g. You do not want an employee pleading with the Board at a public meeting to rescind the resignation letter, as that can become a political spectacle. The employee should plead their case to you, and you have the authority to recommend rescinding the letter of resignation and to inform the board at their next meeting.

h. To attend all Board meetings, closed sessions (including closed session to evaluate the performance of the Superintendent), study sessions, ad hoc meetings of Board members and all Board committee meetings, except a closed session to discuss termination of the Superintendent.

Note 14h. You want language stating that you will be in closed sessions regarding your *evaluation* so that you can hear from each individual board member as to how they are thinking about your performance. In this way you can respond to their needs and concerns more effectively.

There are those superintendents who spend most of their time with the care and feeding of board members. I do not advocate this approach. I advocate having a strong personal direction for education and spending most of your time implementing it. If you take care of students and staff the community will tend to re-elect board members as you are doing the job they desire. You look for this alignment.

    i.   To review all policies adopted by the Board and make appropriate recommendations to the Board.

    j.   To evaluate employees as provided for by state law or Board policy.

Note 14j. Put diligence into annually evaluating your staff. It is a learning tool and a motivation tool. Every 5 years (my rule of thumb) write a letter of recommendation citing all the things they have done that are of value to you. They will appreciate the recognition.

    k.   To maintain and improve professional competence by all available means: journals, conferences, associations and their activities.

Note 14k. It is the skill and knowledge of staff that is most critical to become an effective District. Put your money here for you and for staff. Avoid *only* allowing in state travel; sometimes it is cheaper to travel out of state than within state. You want the leadership message that you and staff are expected to go anywhere to find the best practices, programs or products to advance education while remaining financially solvent.

l.   To participate in community activities.

Note 14l. Prior to signing the contract, have the board stipulate the superintendent must attend events. If you don't attend their important events, it will become an issue. Conversely, if you spend an inordinate amount of time on activities the board could care less about, you might consider a better use of your time. It is about communication.

    m.   To serve as the liaison between the Board and all employer-employee matters and make recommendations to the Board concerning these matters.

15.   **Board Responsibilities:** The Board's primary responsibility is to govern the organization by formulating and adopting Board policy to establish District direction. They shall provide oversight and accountability of the Superintendent and delegate decision-making with clarity and monitor the Superintendent's job performance.

Note 15.

The board may require an annual physical to determine your fitness for duty, to prove you can do the job. If they push this, I recommend the following language: "If the superintendent receives an annual physical and is rated "Fit for Duty" the board shall compensate the superintendent $1000 per year."

Some Board members will push to not define *their* job in your contract. Hold firm and state that you want to work as a team, and an effective team understands each other's role. so you would prefer to know what you can count on from the board.

    a.   The Board shall identify and reserve for itself any decision they do not want the Superintendent to make.

Note 15a. Use the example, "Is there a principal you do not want me to transfer to another school in the district?" This requires the board to think through their personal favorites and inform you of such.

b. The Board shall not direct the Superintendent to take an action that violates the authority of the Superintendent as stated within this contract.

c. The Board agrees to abide by the Protocols attached to this contract.

d. The Board shall not take any action; adopt any policy, by-law, or regulation which impairs or reduces the duties and authority of the Superintendent as mentioned above under Superintendent Duties.

e. The Board agrees they have vetted the Superintendent well enough to understand and respect that her/his skill and knowledge of leadership and management systems is an asset and commodity of the district.

Note 15e. Ideally the board will know how they want the superintendent to lead the district. This is usually either autocratic (top down) or collaborative. There are a few board members who want option 3. They just want you to do as they tell you to do. It would be wise at the end of the interview, when they ask if you have any questions of the board, to ask, "How do you want me to lead the district?" If they stumble with this question it should be a red flag warning to you that they are not a team, and you will need to focus on creating board teamwork.

f. The Board will inform the Superintendent at the annual evaluation meeting of how they want the District to be managed or not to be managed, and the direction they want for the District.

16. **Board Policy Direction Defined:** School Board Policy direction is a set of written and Board approved guidelines placed in a Board policy manual to provide clear direction to management personnel on what they want accomplished and the parameters of how they want administration to accomplish them. The Policy Manual is a Board framework to hold management accountable to achieve Board goals and objectives within the parameters of the Policy Manual.

Note 16. I suggest researching The Aspen Group Int. "Policy is *not* any action the Board directs the superintendent to do!"

A Board functions best when it sets very clear strategic direction: expectations, goals and objectives for the Superintendent. The Superintendent will then devise a plan to marshal resources, assign personnel, make decisions and regularly communicate the plan to the Board to accomplish the Board's direction. The Board's role focuses on:

♦ Monitoring results

♦ Monitoring how management is keeping the Board informed so that the Board never feels removed from what the management team is doing and how they are making their decisions

♦ Monitoring how management is implementing Board policy

♦ Monitoring administrative efficiency to reduce costs and improve student learning

♦ Monitoring compliance with state and federal regulations

♦ Evaluating performance

> A Board becomes dysfunctional when it, individually or collectively, engages in directing the day to day decisions and operational detail of running a district that interferes or countermands a Superintendent's decisions. Communication between the Board and Superintendent is essential to the success of a District. Knowing who has final authority to make a decision is a necessity for the Superintendent to manage effectively.

Note 16. One common area of board complaint is the superintendent's lack of follow-up and follow through regarding their individual issues. Communication is important; always stay mindful of individual board member issues. Treat the board as a team and show respect for their individual differences and needs.

17. **Performance Objectives:** At an annual evaluation the Board and the superintendent shall *mutually agree* to performance objectives for the year. The Board and superintendent shall mutually agree to an evaluation instrument by May 1 of each year.

18. **Evaluation:** The Board will annually evaluate the superintendent's performance using *mutually agreed* upon objectives for the evaluation. The Board requires the superintendent to provide a written analysis of evidence in meeting the performance objectives prior to the Board reaching final agreement on the evaluation. The Board will submit a written evaluation of the superintendent's performance to her/him on or before July 1st of each year. The evaluation will only reflect progress on the agreed upon objectives between the Board and the Superintendent and

that are so stipulated in an annual amendment to this contract. *A satisfactory evaluation occurs when a majority of the Board votes, in closed session, at a regularly scheduled Board meeting, that the Superintendent's performance of Board goals and objectives is satisfactory; and it is then reported out in open session.*

Note 18. Do not accept language that states the board shall decide the objectives and the board shall decide the evaluation instrument. It is a board-superintendent team. Stay focused on this point.

Acceptable language is *mutually agreed* upon objectives and *mutually agreed* upon evaluation instrument. You want to ask yourself, "Does this evaluation instrument motivate me to do my best work?" If it doesn't, you need to inform the board during the discussion the type of evaluation instrument that would motivate you to do your best work.

19.   Prior to Superintendent evaluation the Board shall conduct a third party facilitated Board self-evaluation. The criteria shall be determined by the Board.

20.   The Board will submit a written evaluation of the Superintendent's performance to her/him on or before July 1st of each year. The evaluation will only reflect progress on the agreed upon objectives between the Board and the Superintendent and that are so stipulated in an annual amendment to this contract.

21.   Reporting on progress: Every 4 months the Superintendent shall report to the Board, in closed session, progress on meeting evaluation objectives.

Note 21. This is critical to make certain you and the Board are in agreement as to the objectives. You might get a Board member who states, "We need to pay attention to something else." Your appropriate response would be to ask the full Board, "What objective would you like me to stop working on?" Point out to the Board that you have created a plan, marshalled resources, and assigned people to accomplish the objectives. If they want to change course mid-stream it can be done, but at the expense of what? Communication is key.

22. **Mentoring:** The Superintendent shall be provided 5 days of mentoring during the first year of this contract. The Superintendent shall select the mentor.

23. In the absence of a formal Board evaluation and absence of Board formal written criticisms, suggestions or reprimands the performance of the Superintendent shall be deemed satisfactory. On or before June 1 the Superintendent shall inform the Board of their timeline to evaluate the Superintendent's performance and the consequence if they do not.

24. **Savings Clause:** If any word, phrase, clause, sentence, paragraph, section or any other part of this contract are held to be contrary to law by final legislative act or a federal or state court of competent jurisdiction, inclusive of appeals, shall be found illegal or unenforceable the remainder of the contract shall continue in full force and effect.

_____

Signatures of the Superintendent and Board of Trustees

Final Notes. Make certain to note any questions or concerns you have and to seek advice from AASA for national superintendents prior to signing the final contract. Remember to practice *patience.*

Remember, just because you are told "no" to an item, this doesn't mean no. First ask *why,* and follow up by stating, "I believe the board can do better than this; how can we resolve the board's issue?" Persistence is the key to success in negotiating a contract, as well as success as a superintendent.

There is always more you can add to your contract, but it is essential to seriously consider what is most important to you. Then be persistent and negotiate with absolute resolution for what you know you need to be a successful leader.

Always ask other superintendents what they have in their contract that they think is important. You can pick up great ideas.

There are superintendents who make things happen,

Others watch what happens,

A few wonder what happened.

The curtain just opened and the lights are blinding,

You're on the leadership stage, it's time to make things happen!

It's all about the contract.

Now – let's go ask the "bear to dance!"

CHAPTER 13

CLEAN SAMPLE CONTRACT WITHOUT NOTES

SUPERINTENDENT EMPLOYMENT CONTRACT

BETWEEN THE BOARD OF TRUSTEES OF THE XYZ SCHOOL DISTRICT AND SUPERINTENDENT

This contract is entered into as of this 1st day of July 20__, between the Board of Trustees (hereinafter referred to as the "Board") of and on behalf of the XYZ School District, (hereinafter referred to as the "District") and Superintendent (hereinafter referred to as the "Superintendent").

Now therefore the above named parties hereby mutually agree as follows:

BOARD- SUPERINTENDENT BELIEF STATEMENT

1. The Board has one employee—the superintendent, and the Board believes a high-performing Board-superintendent team has the greatest impact on student education because of the authority vested in these positions. Teamwork is not sharing decisions between the Board and the superintendent it is sharing complimentary yet separate roles.

The Board knows the position of superintendent has the highest turnover rate in education, making it the most vulnerable position within the district. For these reasons, the Board believes it is necessary to clearly define the duties of the Superintendent and the Board to serve as a basis for effective communication and teamwork in the management of the school district. By doing so the Board believes this will enhance Superintendent stability, longevity, and effectiveness, improving the overall quality of the educational program and the operational success of the district. **Superintendent, Chief Executive Officer of the Governing Board, Secretary for the Board:** Superintendent is employed as the Superintendent of the School District. (S)He shall also be the Chief Executive Officer of the Governing Board and shall serve as the secretary for the Board.

2. **Term:** ___ years. Beginning July 1, 20__, the Board employs the Superintendent for a period of ___ years terminating on June 30, 20__.

3. **Reassignment:** The Superintendent is employed specifically and solely to perform the duties as Superintendent of schools for the district. The Superintendent cannot be reassigned from the position as Superintendent to another position without the Superintendent's written authorization.

4. **Amendment of Agreement:** This agreement shall only be changed, modified or amended by mutual consent of the parties.

5. **Contract Renewal:** On or before March 15, 20__ the Superintendent shall submit to the Board a new contract proposal. The Board will have until June 15, 20__, to respond to the proposal. If the Board does not respond to the proposal, the current terms and conditions remain in effect until the contract's termination date.

If the Superintendent receives a satisfactory evaluation the contract shall be extended for one year and acted upon at the next regularly scheduled Board meeting in the form of an amendment to the contract.

6. **Intellectual Property:** Any and all inventions, discoveries, developments, innovations, programs or practices conceived by the Superintendent relative to the duties under this agreement shall be the exclusive property of the Superintendent.

7. **Consulting/ Conflict of interest:** The Superintendent shall be permitted to undertake consulting, writing, teaching, and speaking engagements so long as these do not interfere with the performance of the duties as Superintendent. Any consulting work undertaken by the Superintendent for compensation must be taken on vacation days, personal days, holidays or non-duty days. The Superintendent shall comply with regulations regarding a conflict of interest. The aforementioned prohibition shall include, without limitation holding a pecuniary (financial) interest in any property, product or service provided to or being considered to be provided to the District.

8. **Termination Without Cause:** The Board may terminate this Agreement with a super-majority vote of the Board at a regularly scheduled Board meeting. If the Board seeks to terminate this contract, the cash and benefit settlement shall be the amount of time left on the contract or the maximum allowed by law, whichever is less. The buyout provision remains in force if the Superintendent secures other employment within the amount of time left on the contract. If the Board exercises **Termination Without Cause** they agree they shall not speak negatively about the Superintendent in any public or private meeting. This is defined as a meeting between one or more people or on social media.

9. **Termination for Just Cause:** The Superintendent shall only be terminated for just cause. Should the Board elect to pursue Termination for Just Cause; the Board must first provide Superintendent with a statement detailing the incidents of malfeasance and give Superintendent six months to demonstrate improvement. If the Board elects the option to terminate this Agreement with just cause, it must do so by taking action at a **regularly scheduled board** meeting with a **supermajority vote** of the Board.

10. **Abuse of Power/Termination for Cause:** Abuse of power: If the Superintendent is placed on paid leave or her/his legal defense in a criminal trial is paid by the District and (s)he is subsequently convicted of abusing her/his office or her/his title (s)he must reimburse the District for her/his criminal defense.

11. **New Position:** The Superintendent must notify the Board President whenever **offered a contract** for a new position.

12. **Salary/Work Year/Vacation Days:** The annual base salary for 20_-20_ shall be $$$$$$ with a work year of 223 days and 24 vacation days, exclusive of legal holidays as per the management team salary schedule.

WORK YEAR FORMULA

Days in Year = 365
– 104 weekend days
= 261 possible work days

– 14 paid holidays (*depending on specific district*)
= 247 possible work days

– 24 vacation days (*depending on specific contract*)
= 223 work days (*depending on specific contract*)

Sample Superintendent contract formula from Association of California School Administrators

a. The Superintendent's salary and/or work year cannot be reduced **unless every employee** in the District has had their salary and/or work year reduced.

b. The salary shall be paid in equal monthly installments.

c. The Board reserves the right to otherwise adjust the Superintendent's compensation. Any adjustment in compensation during the term of this Contract shall be only in the form of an amendment and only as mutually agreed to by and between the parties, and shall not operate as a termination of this Contract. It is further provided that, with respect to any adjustment in salary, it shall not be considered that a new Contract has been entered into or that the termination date of the existing contract has been extended

d. The Superintendent can bank/save any and all unused vacation days and be reimbursed at her/his daily rate of pay for any unused vacation days. Her/ His daily rate is determined by dividing her/his annual base salary by her/his work year (223). The amount of vacation days carried over shall be at the sole discretion of the Superintendent.

13. **Fringe Benefits:** The Superintendent shall be accorded such fringe benefits of employment as are granted to the District's "management team" employees and:

a. Technology: To maintain effective communication the district shall provide a cell phone for business and personal use and full use of all forms of technology of the Superintendent's choice (including, but not limited to, computers, tablet devices, printers, fax machines, cellular and data services, etc.) plus all related charges and expenses for personal and business use.

b. Expenses: The Superintendent shall be provided a District credit card for actual and necessary expenses incurred within the scope of employment while representing the district. Except as herein provided, the District shall provide reimbursement to the Superintendent for all actual and necessary business-related expenses as paid by the Superintendent in the conduct of her/his duties and on behalf of the District.

c. Automobile: The District shall provide the Superintendent a mutually agreeable automobile for her/his personal and professional use. The District agrees to provide a District credit card for the Superintendent to use for gas and emergency maintenance of the vehicle. The District agrees to keep the automobile maintained in good working condition and provide insurance coverage for the vehicle.

d. Professional Organizations/Conferences/Education: The Board shall pay for the expenses for the Superintendent as CEO to participate in professional organizations, conferences and activities at the local, county, state, and national level at the discretion of the Superintendent. The Board shall pay the Superintendent's related membership dues, fees, and expenses accordingly. The Board shall receive an annual accounting of all expenses.

e. Sick/Personal leave (credited in advance): The Superintendent shall accrue 2 days of sick leave per month, or 24 per year; 10 of which can be used as personal leave. As a continuation of benefits earned from her/his prior employer, the Superintendent shall receive a sick leave credit with the District for any and all unused accumulated leave from her/his prior employer. Said continuation benefit shall be added to the Superintendent's sick leave benefit in the first year of this agreement. The continuation benefit shall accrue upon submission of proper evidence from the prior employer of entitlement benefits.

f. Health and Welfare Benefits: The Superintendent shall be provided the same coverage as management team employees of the District.

g. Life Insurance: The District shall pay 5% of Superintendent's base salary per year for life insurance for the Superintendent. The Superintendent shall select the life insurance as well as the beneficiaries.

h. Tax Sheltered Account (TSA): The District shall pay 5% of base salary for a fully vested TSA of the Superintendent's choice.

i. Relocation Expense: The District shall pay $20,000 for the Superintendent to relocate within the District.

j. Housing Allowance: The District shall pay $2,000 per month for the life of the contract for the Superintendent to use for housing within the District.

k. Professional Liability/ Hold Harmless: If the Superintendent is named personally in a legal action as a result of duties undertaken on behalf of the District, the Board agrees to defend and hold harmless and indemnify the Superintendent from all demands, suits, claims, actions and legal proceedings- excluding the abuse of power clause of this contract. Legal defense shall be determined pursuant to Government Code section 995 *et seq.* In no case will individual Board members be considered personally liable for indemnifying the Superintendent against such demands, claims, suits, actions and legal proceedings.

l. Contract Retirement Audit: The District shall *fully indemnify* and provide mutually agreeable legal defense in the event of an audit of the Superintendent's employment contract or retirement income. In no case shall individual Board members be considered personally liable for indemnifying the Superintendent against such demands, claims, suits, actions and legal proceedings.

14. **Superintendent Duties:** The Superintendent's primary responsibility is to manage the District to implement the policy direction of the Board. The Superintendent shall be governed by and perform duties and respon-

sibilities set forth in the laws of the State of __, formal duties as defined within this contract and by rules, regulations, policies, and advice and direction of the Board.

In discharging the Superintendent authority (s)he shall keep the Board informed with follow up and follow through communication so that the Board understands the why and how of decisions.

a. To not act on individual Board member direction as this is a violation of the contract and grounds for termination of employment.

b. To manage the day to day decisions of the district to institute reforms and systemic changes as the Superintendent finds necessary in order to achieve the Boards direction, goals, and objectives.

c. To organize or reorganize the administrative and all management staff which in her/his judgment best serves the district.

d. To assign principals to their schools and transfer or demote existing personnel.

e. To administer all programs; funds; personnel; facilities; contracts; and all other administrative and academic functions.

f. To recommend all new employees to the District or employees new to their position to the Board for their approval. The Board reserves the authority to accept or reject the Superintendent's recommendation to hire new personnel. If the Board rejects the Superintendent's final recommendation the Superintendent has the authority to make a new recommendation until it meets with Board approval.

♦ The Superintendent recommends employees

♦ The Board has final authority to approve employees

g. To immediately accept employee resignations for and on behalf of the Board. The resignation is final once the Superintendent signs and dates receipt of all resignations. The Superintendent shall inform the Board of all resignations at the next regular Board meeting as a personnel information item.

h. To attend all Board meetings, closed sessions *(including closed session to evaluate the performance of the Superintendent),* study sessions, ad hoc meetings of Board members, and all Board committee meetings except a closed session to discuss termination of the Superintendent.

i. To review all policies adopted by the Board and make appropriate recommendations to the Board.

j. To evaluate employees as provided for by state law or Board policy.

k. To maintain and improve professional competence by all available means: journals, conferences, associations and their activities.

l. To participate in community activities.

m. To serve as the liaison between the Board and all employer-employee matters and make recommendations to the Board concerning these matters.

15. **Board Responsibilities:** The Board's primary responsibility is to govern the organization by formulating and adopting Board policy to establish District direction. They shall provide oversight and accountability of the Superintendent and delegate decision-making with clarity and monitor the Superintendent's job performance.

a. The Board shall identify and reserve for itself any decision they do not want the Superintendent to make.

b. The Board shall not direct the Superintendent to take an action that violates the authority of the Superintendent as stated within this contract.

c. The Board agrees to abide by the Protocols attached to this contract.

d. The Board shall not take any action; adopt any policy, by-law or regulation which impairs or reduces the duties and authority of the Superintendent as mentioned above under Superintendent Duties.

e. The Board agrees they have vetted the Superintendent well enough to understand and respect that her/his skill and knowledge of leadership and management systems is an asset and commodity of the district.

f. The Board will inform the Superintendent at the annual evaluation meeting of how they want the District to be managed or not to be managed, and the direction they want for the District.

16. **Board Policy Direction Defined:** School Board Policy direction is a set of written and Board approved guidelines placed in a Board policy manual to provide clear direction to management personnel on what they want accomplished and the parameters of how they want administration to accomplish them. The Policy Manual is a Board framework to hold management accountable to achieve Board goals and objectives within the parameters of the Policy Manual.

A Board functions best when it sets very clear strategic direction: expectations, goals and objectives for the Superintendent. The Superintendent will then devise a plan to marshal resources, assign personnel, make decisions and regularly communicate the plan to the Board to accomplish the Board's direction. The Board's role focuses on:

- ◆ Monitoring results

- ◆ Monitoring how management is keeping the Board informed, so that the Board never feels removed from what the management team is doing and how they are making their decisions

- ◆ Monitoring how management is implementing Board policy

- ◆ Monitoring administrative efficiency to reduce costs and improve student learning

  - ○ Monitoring compliance with state and federal regulations

  - ○ Evaluating performance

17. **Performance Objectives:** At an annual evaluation the Board and the Superintendent shall **mutually agree** to performance objectives for the year. The Board and Superintendent shall mutually agree to an evaluation instrument by May 1 of each year.

18. **Evaluation:** The Board will annually evaluate the Superintendent's performance using **mutually agreed** upon objectives for the evaluation. The Board requires the Superintendent to provide written analysis of evidence in meeting the performance objectives prior to the Board reaching fin analysis of evidence in meeting the performance objectives prior to the Board reaching final agreement on the evaluation. The Board shall submit a written evaluation of the Superintendent's performance to her/him on or before July 1st of each year. The evaluation shall only reflect progress on the agreed upon objectives between the Board and the Superintendent and that are so stipulated in an annual amendment to this contract. **A satisfactory evaluation occurs when a majority of the Board votes, in**

closed session, at a regularly scheduled Board meeting that the Superintendents performance of Board goals and objectives is satisfactory; and is then reported out in open session.

a. Prior to Superintendent evaluation the Board shall conduct a third party facilitated Board self-evaluation. The criteria shall be determined by the Board.

b. The Board will submit a written evaluation of the Superintendent's performance to her/him on or before July 1st of each year. The evaluation will only reflect progress on the agreed upon objectives between the Board and the Superintendent and that are so stipulated in an annual amendment to this contract.

c. Reporting on progress: Every 4 months the Superintendent shall report to the Board, in closed session, progress on meeting evaluation objectives.

d. In the absence of a formal Board evaluation and absence of Board formal written criticisms, suggestions or reprimands the performance of the Superintendent shall be deemed satisfactory.

e. If the Superintendent is rated as satisfactory the Board shall take action at the next regularly scheduled Board meeting to extend the Superintendent's contract by one year.

f. The contract extension shall be in the form of an amendment to the contract.

g. On or before June 1 the Superintendent shall inform the Board of their timeline to evaluate the Superintendent's performance and the consequence if they do not.

19. **Mentoring:** The Superintendent shall be provided 5 days of mentoring during the first year of this contract. The Superintendent shall select the mentor and approved by the Board.

20. **Savings Clause:** If any word, phrase, clause, sentence, paragraph, section or any other part of this contract are held to be contrary to law by final legislative act or a federal or state court of competent jurisdiction, inclusive of appeals, shall be found illegal or unenforceable the remainder of the contract shall continue in full force and effect.

_____

Signatures of the Superintendent and Board of Trustees

REFERENCES

Abrashoff, M. *It's Your Ship.* New York:Warner Books, 2002.

Almond, J., Morey, J., Dezutti, S., Tschida, B., Todd, R., Jones, J., and Wamhof, L., "Ten Tips to Know Before Signing the First Superintendent Contract". *ACSA EdCal.* 2016.

Association of California School Administrators. *Superintendent Sample Contract.* Superintendents' Symposium. Monterey, CA. 2010.

Bader and Associates. *7 Questions Great Boards Ask,* 2008, www. GreatBoards.org.

Bassi, L. and McMurrer, D., "Maximizing Your Return On People," *Harvard Business Review*, 2007.

Bennis, W., "The Leadership Advantage," *Leader to Leader.* No. 12, Spring 1999, 18-23.

Berliner, D. *Expertise in Teaching: How It Develops and What It Looks Like.* Lecture, School of Education, University of California at Riverside. 1999.

Blanchard, K. *The High Cost of Doing Nothing.* Ken Blanchard Companies. 2009.

Buckingham, M. and Coffman, C. *First Break All the Rules.* New York: Simon & Schuster. 1999.

Canfield, J. *The Success Principles.* New York: Harper Collins. 2005.

Caplan, L. *The Role of Superintendent Tenure on Student Achievement in Selected School Districts In New York State* (EdD dissertation, Sage Graduate School of Education, 2010).

Clifton, J. *The Coming Jobs War*. New York: Gallup Press, 2011.

Covey, S. M. R. *The Speed of Trust*. New York: Free Press, 2006:

Collins, J. *Good to Great*. New York: Harper Collins, 2001.

California School Boards Association. *Superintendent Contract Template*. Annotated Version. 2016

Dawson, L. and Quinn, R. *Clarifying Board Superintendent Roles*. AASA:*The School Administrator*. 2000.

Deming, W.E. *Essential Principals of TQM*. 2016. People.well.com

Dickinson, E. "I'm Nobody! Who Are You?," 1891.

Finnen, L. and McCord, R. *AASA 2017-2018 Superintendent Salary Benefit Study*. AASA. 2018

Frost, R. "The Road Not Taken," 1916.

Giang, V. *7 Tips to Win Any Negotiation*. 2018. www.americanexpress.com.

Goitia, E. *The Ultimate Contract Negotiation Guide*, Promo Rockstars. http://www.promorockstar.com/group.

Goulston, M. . *Just Listen*. Amacom American Management Association. 2009.

Grissom, J.A. and Andersen, S., "Why Superintendents Turn Over" *American Educational Research Journal*. Vol. 49 (2012).

Hargreaves, A. and Fink, D. "The Seven Principles of Sustainable Leadership" *Educational Leadership*, April, 2004, Vol. 6, No. 7.

Hedges, K. "Six Surprising Negotiation Tactics That Get You the Best Deal," *Forbes Woman*, 2018. www.forbes.com.

Hill, P. and Jochim, A. *Unlocking Potential: How Political Skill Can Maximize Superintendent Effectiveness*. Center for Reinventing Public Education. 2018.

Investopedia. www.investopedia.com.

Johnson, D. and Johnson, F. *Joining Together: Group Theory And Group Skills*. Boston: Allyn & Bacon, 2000.

Kipling, Rudyard. *"If," 1910.*

Lafferty, C. . *Lifestyles Inventory*. Presentation. ACSA invitational conference, Newport Beach, CA. 1989.

Levering, R. *A. Great Place to Work*. New York: Random House, 1988.

Lewis, A. *Effective Superintendents, Effective Boards: Finding the Right Fit*. Special Report Educational Writers Association, 2003.

Lezotte, L. *Effective Schools*. Lecture. Victorville, CA, 2010.

Lopez, S. *Making Hope Happen*. New York: Atria Books, 2013.

Madden, J. *Top Twenty-Five Quotes by John Madden*. www.azquotes. com .

Mayer, R. *How Not to be A Terrible School Board Member*. Thousand Oaks, CA: Corwin, 2011.

McColl, A. "Critical Choices in Superintendent Contracts." *School Law Bulletin*, 2000, *Vol.31, No. 2.*

Metzger, C., "Search for Meaning." *The Lens, A Quarterly E-Newsletter/Journal; Center for Empowered Leadership,* issue 14 (2010). www.cfel.org/lens14christa.html.

Montgomery, R. . *Life Insurance Overview*. Presentation. Hesperia Unified School District, CA., 2016.

Mountford, M., "Motives and Power of School Board Members: Implications for School Board-Superintendent Relationships." *Educational Administration Quarterly* Vol. 40, No. 5. (2004). http:// eaq.sagepub.com/cgi/content/abstract/40/5/704, http://www. sagepublications.com.

Nielsen, D. *Every School: One Citizen's Guide to Transforming*

Education. Seattle Discovery Institute Press, 2014.

Nisen, M. "14 Surprising Tricks to Boost Your Salary," 2014, www.businessinsider.com.

Pink, D. *Drive*, Riverhead Books; New York: Penguin Group, 2009.

Plotts, T. (2011) *A Multiple Regression Analysis of Factors Concerning Superintendent Longevity and Continuity Relative to Student Achievement.* (EdD dissertation, Seton Hall University, 2011).

Quinn, R. and Dawson, L. *Good Governance is A Choice.* Lanham, Maryland: Rowan & Littlefield Publishing, 2011.

Quinn, R. *Deep Change.* Jossey-Bass, 1996.

Robertson, K. *5 Ways to Negotiate More Effectively.* Small Business: Canada, 2014. www.about.com.

Stim, R. *Contract Negotiations: 11 Strategies.* NOLO Law for All. www.nolo.com.

Terez, T. Build a Better Workplace. *A Working White Paper: Power Over Vs Power With.* 2010. BuildaBetterworkplace.com.

Tzu, Sun. *The Art of War,* annotated English version , 2010. Wikipedia.com.

Virginia Department of Education. *Guidelines For Uniform Performance Standards And Evaluation Criteria For Superintendents.* Richmond Virginia, 2010.

Waters, T., Marzano, R., and McNulty, B.. *School Leadership That Works.* Alexandria: ASCD, 2005.

Waters, T. and Marzano, R. *School District Leadership That Works: the Effect of Superintendent Leadership on Student Achievement: A Working Paper.* McRel., 2006.

Wong, H. *There Is Only One Way to Improve Student Achievement.* Presentation, Effective Schools Conference, Scottsdale Arizona, 1999.

Yee, G., and Cuban, L. "When Is Tenure Long Enough? A Historical Analysis of Superintendent Turnover and Tenure In Urban School Districts." *Educational Administration Quarterly*. Vol. 32., No. 1 (1996).

Zuieback, S. and Dalmau, T. *Facilitation Skills for Chaotic Times*. Presentation, Desert Mountain SELPA, Victorville Ca. 2006.

AFTERWORD

My desire in writing this book was to advise up-and-coming superintendents on the importance of a comprehensive contract as well as to warn them of mistakes I made in negotiating my final contract. The mistakes resulted in a contract controversy with much negative media attention.

A retired superintendent friend, Dr. Dennis Byas, spoke with me at the end of the controversy and stated, "Ralph, nobody survives what you survived. You need to explain how you did it."

HOW WE DID IT

The quick summary is that in my first year as a superintendent the Board directed me to dismiss a principal. By February of my first year I concurred, and recommended he be reassigned to the classroom. Instead of going back to the classroom he retired early. He then ran for a vacant board seat and was elected on his second attempt. His first task was to go after my fringe benefits in my contract. I bent to his bullying and removed a board paid $12,000 per year TSA. The loss to me over time was a minimum of $265,000, not including interest. *This mistake was on me!*

FINAL CONTRACT

When I negotiated my final contract, the Board president stated the Board would back anything I wanted to reward me for our accomplishments under my leadership. I told her *I wanted what I had given up years earlier.*

My rogue board member refused to agree to anything and promised to ruin my career and his fellow board member's re-elections.

FIRST MISTAKE

I lived by the rule to never show anger towards a board member. Well, I broke that rule big time, and I lost it with this guy — because he refuted all the good work the staff had accomplished. I couldn't take another moment of him refusing to admit the good work we had accomplished, and I exploded on him. On a straw vote he finally realized the vote was a strong 4-1 in favor of my contract. He baited me, and I fell for it when he suggested, "Why hide your fringe benefit income? Why not put it all on salary?"

I said,"OK." I did fold it into salary. That was a huge mistake, as the local press ran with that story. *I never developed a media message.* He contacted our local newspaper editor with his side of the story. When the media contacted me I was all over the place without a clear concise message. I should have stuck to one message no matter what I was asked, "I appreciate the board's confidence in my ability to lead our district."

FAILURE TO ACKNOWLEDGE THE POLITICAL LANDSCAPE

As I recall, our governor supported four propositions on the upcoming November ballot that united teachers and nurses. Politics were in the air, and I didn't pay attention. One of our past teacher union presidents was trying to get his wife elected as the new union president (she lost that election) and he organized some staff against me. Protest was in the air.

FAILURE TO NEGOTIATE TEACHERS CONTRACT BEFORE MINE

We had to make a change in our salary schedule as a result of a wage issue in the middle columns of our salary schedule with teachers. It was simply out of line with our local school districts. The ex-teachers union president rallied some staff, as I was separating myself from them by asking for more than what I gave them.

I should have negotiated their contract first, and corrected the salary schedule mistake.

REASON FOR OUR SUCCESS

The board and I had at that time successfully led a district for 20 years and the community supported us. A board member noticed that of all the negative comments in the "Letters to the Editor" section of our local paper were *not* from our school district. (At that time you could track online the location of the comments made.)

RENEGOTIATED MY CONTRACT

At one packed board meeting I announced we would re-negotiate the contract and reach an agreement that night, and we did so.

A SINCERE APOLOGY TO STAFF

The contract dispute occurred at the end of the year. At the beginning of the new school year I addressed all staff and apologized for seeking "too much, too soon."

VINDICATION

The local paper had touted our rogue board member as the most "sane" board member within our community. He received tremendous free press. That November, at the next board election, the results spoke *loudly*:

The rogue board member not only lost but he came in dead last. The voters spoke—thank you, thank you, and thank you again!

Three years later, in my last year as superintendent, our community passed a local General Obligation Bond that would provide school facilities for years to come for our staff and students. How did we survive?

Good work speaks for itself.

Appendix A

SAMPLE PRESS RELEASE

MEDIA MESSAGE FROM BOARD

XYZ School District Board of Trustees
Superintendent Compensation Community Report

As a school board, we believe our primary task is to attract and retain the most qualified and competent superintendent. We have unanimously selected Dr. John Doe as our superintendent. As a Board we have been able to observe, monitor, and evaluate Dr. John Doe's job performance and fit with our community. As a Board we have judged him to be an outstanding leader.

The final phase in retaining a successful superintendent is negotiating an appropriate and fair contract, and it is a challenging task. As school board members we balance the desire to retain competent leadership with the need to rein in costs for taxpayers and to justify a compensation package to district employees and the community at large. Over the last several years we have had many superintendent changes that adversely affected our school system and community. We have found the right leader and negotiated his contract with the mindset to retain his services to provide stability to our school district.

Superintendents face a highly challenging workload that requires a broad skill set. There have been times when members of the public state that they do not understand the role of the superintendent. They feel that all district funding should be focused on classroom teachers, neglecting the critical role that credentialed support staff, classified employees, and administrative personnel play in providing a high-quality education to our community's children.

We as a Board, however, could not ignore what the research and experience of other districts has shown us: without a strong superintendent, the positive work of individual teachers and principals does not spread system-wide. Student achievement levels do not progress, district-wide staff morale drops, the reputations of local schools suffer, and it becomes still harder to hire quality staff—all leading to a perpetual downward cycle, which not only is bad for a community's children, but is also bad for a local economy. Companies and families will not choose to locate in communities with poorly performing public schools.

QUALITY SCHOOLS INCREASE HOUSING VALUES

Simply said, a quality superintendent who builds a quality educational system will have a positive effect on increasing housing values over time.

TERMS AND CONDITIONS OF NEW CONTRACT REACHED

The board and superintendent have successfully reached agreement on the terms and conditions of a new four year contract. We are absolutely delighted that the superintendent has agreed to assume the leadership of our district.

LEADERSHIP MATTERS

As we began the contract negotiating process the first question we had to ask ourselves is how important a superintendent is in the overall achievement levels for students. In fact, many research studies have shown that superintendents do have a strong effect on student achievement, either positive or negative. To draw from just one of them, "School District Leadership that Works," the authors Waters and Marzano made significant findings:

♦ District leadership matters

♦ Effective superintendents focus their efforts on creating goal-oriented districts

♦ Superintendent longevity is positively correlated with student achievement

In fact, this study stated, *"The longevity of the superintendent has twice the impact on student achievement than any other comprehensive school reform."*

It is no accident, therefore, that state and national school board support organizations such as the California School Boards Association emphasize that one of the board's most critical roles is to hire and supervise the superintendent. An ideal contract is one that will help the district retain the most effective superintendent and promote an extended tenure in the district.

BROADER ISSUES IN HIRING SUPERINTENDENTS

The superintendent market nationally is a difficult one: a 2006 American Association of School Administrators study showed that 80 percent of superintendents were at retirement age and were part of the Baby Boomer generation. The younger cohort of rising administrators is part of Generation X, a numerically smaller group of possible employees. Across the country, it is also a time of great stress on school budgets, with a corresponding negative effect on employee morale across all levels of the district—including the superintendent. Employees who were drawn to helping children discover that that people and programs that benefit students must be cut again and again. On average, superintendents stay in their positions for three years.

CONSIDERATIONS

We decided to offer a salary of $$$$$$, which we believe is a wise investment for our district's future. Leadership matters, and we pay for what we get. We wanted a quality leader. The superintendent is the board's only employee, and as such, we offered a competitive compensation package in recognition of his/ her demonstrated leadership skill. We included contract language that provides for strong assessment and evaluation cycles based on district goals.

We recognized the superintendent would be a highly desirable candidate in other districts. We are extremely pleased for our district and our community that we have been able to retain a leader who has the capabilities to ensure quality schools and quality education for the children, families, and the community we serve.

Source: Santa Barbara Unified School District Superintendent Compensation Report 2011

Appendix B

EVALUATION

I've never heard a superintendent say, "I have an excellent evaluation instrument."

In my opinion, the reason is pretty basic. How do we create a *professional* evaluation instrument within a *political* system? Board members, in general, feel they can never protect themselves enough from all the possibilities of superintendent problems that they could be asked to address in the media at their next election.

The task is to shape an all-inclusive evaluation system that bridges the Board's concerns with adequate professional protections to allow the superintendent to lead effectively.

Before signing a contract make certain you have evaluation language that states goals and objectives shall be "mutually agreeable." If boards think they need to protect themselves from superintendent issues, then vice versa, superintendents need to think what could go wrong.

A former assistant superintendent was hired by a well-known district. Then he called complaining that the board created new objectives at every board meeting. Everything that he and the superintendent tried to do to get the board focused fell on deaf ears. He left for another district after one year. The superintendent left the following year. Some boards are not effective.

ALL-INCLUSIVE EVALUATION SYSTEM

I prefer to include three areas for evaluation

♦ *Results:* negotiated with the board

♦ *Duties/Responsibilities:* Taken from your negotiated employment contract

♦ *Professional Behavior:* Negotiated with the board

Stay away from numerical scores, as one board member can skew the overall score, and also reject evaluations that use "percentage of objectives met." Make certain that you have language in your contract llowing you to present written evidence of what you accomplished in th year prior to being evaluated by the board. The board votes whether they believe you were satisfactory in completing the objectives, etc., with a simple majority vote.

PURPOSE OF EVALUATION

The purpose of evaluation is to promote superintendent growth and insure accountability. Several states have thorough superintendent evaluation instruments. I always preferred to know what the board wanted accomplished, and from that I would have our management team draft a plan, implement the plan, and monitor progress throughout the year. The board would then evaluate me as to whether or not they thought our progress was "satisfactory".

I get nervous when I observe a detailed evaluation instrument with pages of instructions, as I know it will take considerable time away from my duties as a superintendent. Other superintendents I've known thoroughly enjoy detailed evaluation procedures. It is personal preference. My point is that you need to know your preference and communicate that to the board. Communication is important in working with the board.

SAMPLE EVALUATION

ALL- INCLUSIVE SUPERINTENDENT
EVALUATION CRITERIA

EVALUATION CRITERIA	EXCELLENT	SATISFACTORY	UNSATISFACTORY
Results (As negotiated with the Board) Note: These are generic areas from which objectives would be written.			
1. Achievement			
2. Curriculum			
3. Instruction			
4. Finances			
5. Facilities			
6. School Safety			
7. Public Relations			
8. Staff Relations			

Evaluation Criteria	Excellent	Satisfactory	Unsatisfactory
Superintendent Duties/ Responsibilities (Reflecting negotiated contract language. See sample contract.)			
Manage the day-to-day decisions of the district to implement board policy direction			
Communicate with the board so they understand the why and how of superintendent decisions			
Refrain from acting on individual board member direction			
Assign principals to schools; organize staff to best serve the district, and administer all programs, funds and personnel			
Recommend employees to be hired to the board; accept employee resignations and evaluate employees			
Attend all board meetings/ closed sessions, including evaluation, excluding closed sessions to discuss termination of superintendent.			
Advise the board on all policies			

EVALUATION CRITERIA	EXCELLENT	SATISFACTORY	UNSATISFACTORY
Maintain and improve professional competence			
Participate in community activities			
Serve as the liaison between the board and all employer-employee matters			
Prepare evaluation format for the superintendent's job performance rating and submit to the board			
Professional Behaviors (As negotiated with the Board.)			
Initiative: Has enthusiasm, confidence, and takes initiative to accomplish tasks.			
Perseverance: Focused follow-through to completion on tasks in a positive and constructive manner.			
Productivity: Achieves results consistently.			
Responsibility: Accepts 100% accountability for actions and results without blaming or making excuses.			

Evaluation Criteria	Excellent	Satisfactory	Unsatisfactory
Flexibility: Is respectful and cooperative in difficult situations.			
Teamwork: Utilizes an inclusive and **reflective problem solving** process to create an environment focusing on problem solving the task and not attacking the individual.			
Communication: Listens first for understanding; stays in control of emotions; is direct- factual; speaks with candor and respect. Keeps Board informed of actions and results.			
Social Awareness: Knowing what to say; when to say it and how to say it.			
Overall Rating			

Comments/ Commendations/Other

CPSIA information can be obtained
at www.ICGtesting.com
Printed in the USA
LVHW050932140419
614125LV00041B/2868